Being Franciscan

Being Franciscan

Living the Tradition

Nicholas Alan Worssam SSF

CANTERBURY
PRESS
Norwich

© Nicholas Alan Worssam 2022

Published in 2022 by Canterbury Press
Editorial office
3rd Floor, Invicta House,
108–114 Golden Lane,
London EC1Y OTG, UK

www.canterburypress.co.uk

Canterbury Press is an imprint of Hymns Ancient & Modern Ltd
(a registered charity)

Hymns Ancient & Modern® is a registered trademark of
Hymns Ancient & Modern Ltd
13A Hellesdon Park Road, Norwich,
Norfolk NR6 5DR, UK

British Library Cataloguing in Publication data

A catalogue record for this book is available
from the British Library.

ISBN 978-1-78622-430-9

Typeset by Regent Typesetting
Printed and bound by
CPI Group (UK) Ltd

Contents

Acknowledgements   ix

Foreword by Bishop David Walker   xi

Introduction   1

1 The Founder: Francis of Assisi (1182–1226)   6

2 The Companion: Clare of Assisi (1194–1253)   31

3 The Hermit: Giles of Assisi (1190–1262)   52

4 The Penitent: Margaret of Cortona (1247–1297)   73

5 The Scholar: Bonaventure of Bagnoregio
   (1217/21–1274)   97

6 The Visionary: Angela of Foligno (1248–1309)   125

7 The Poet: Jacopone da Todi (c. 1230–1306)   151

Epilogue   178

Bibliography   185

Appendix: Questions for Reflection and Discussion   192

[Jesus said,] 'Whatever house you enter, first say, "Peace to this house!" And if anyone is there who shares in peace, your peace will rest on that person; but if not, it will return to you.' (Luke 10.5–6)

For the great desire of blessed Francis was that he, as well as his brothers, would abound in such good deeds for which the Lord would be praised. He used to tell them, 'As you announce peace with your mouth, make sure that greater peace is in your hearts. Let no one be provoked to anger or scandal through you, but may everyone be drawn to peace, kindness and harmony through your gentleness. For we have been called to this: to heal the wounded, bind up the broken, and bring others to a knowledge of the truth.'
From *The Legend of the Three Companions*
(*Francis of Assisi: Early Documents*, vol. 2, pp. 101–2)

Acknowledgements

With grateful thanks to those who have read the first drafts of this book, and made invaluable comments and suggestions, especially to Dr Stephanie Cloete, Dr William E. Crozier, Br Joseph Emmanuel SSF, Fr John-Francis Friendship TSSF, and to Christine Smith, Rachel Geddes and all at Canterbury Press.

My thanks also go to my brothers and sisters in the Society of St Francis for their encouragement and support.

I dedicate this book to my parents, Bernard and Beryl. May they rest in peace.

Excerpts from Regis J. Armstrong, J. A. Wayne Hellmann and William J. Short (editors), 1999–2000, *Francis of Assisi: Early Documents* (abbreviated here as *FA:ED*), Volume 1 *The Saint*; Volume 2 *The Founder*; Volume 3 *The Prophet*, Hyde Park, NY: New City Press. Used with permission.

Excerpts from Regis J. Armstrong, 2006, *Clare of Assisi: Early Documents (CA:ED), The Lady*, Hyde Park, NY: New City Press. Used with permission.

Scripture quotations are from the New Revised Standard Version Bible: Anglicized Edition, copyright © 1989, 1995 National Council of the Churches of Christ in the United States of America. Used by permission. All rights reserved worldwide.

Foreword

To be a Christian can never be confused with simple assent to doctrinal principles. It is about following the Jesus whom we believe to be both Son of God and a human being; one who walked this earth 2,000 years ago. Hence, from the very first centuries of the Church, Christians have looked not only to Jesus but to the lives led by those who have appeared to follow him most closely. One such life is that of Francis, the poor man of Assisi, the somewhat accidental founder of one of the great religious movements of the early second millennium. A man whose influence still impacts the lives of so many today; Christians like Brother Nicholas Alan SSF, who seek to 'follow Jesus after the example of St Francis'.

An early challenge for any religious movement is whether and how it continues to grow and flourish beyond the life and leadership of its founder. A movement of the Holy Spirit must always be greater than simply the attractiveness of a charismatic instigator. Here, we read of the lives not only of Francis and his friend and contemporary Clare, but of a handful of Franciscan saints, drawn from the movement's first century, who each exemplified aspects of what it means to follow Jesus after the example of Francis.

Unusually for a founder, Francis resigned leadership of his Order. His calling was not to be the administrator of an institution, but to be an example of this particular form of life to which God was calling women and men. These formed the First Order brothers, the Second Order enclosed sisters, and the Third Order for those with secular responsibilities respectively. The individuals celebrated in this book are likewise exemplars of the Franciscan charism. They are foremost among the people who shaped Franciscan life into the form that has been handed down to us today. These are the people to whom Franciscans such as myself return for guidance and inspiration.

When we look to the great traditions of the Religious or Monastic life in the Western Church, we are inclined to think of them as being shaped primarily by their vows and Rule, as was the earlier Benedictine tradition. Or we turn to their pattern of prayer and discipline, as with the Spiritual Exercises on which Ignatius of Loyola founded the Jesuit movement. The Franciscan tradition indeed has its key vows of poverty, chastity and obedience, and Francis himself wrote various versions of the First Order Rule, which were later revised (some would say watered down) on multiple occasions. Franciscans too have created patterns of prayer, and sought to share them with the wider Church. However, what carries the Franciscan movement forward is much less its documents and disciplines than the lives of its most prominent disciples. Hence the importance of this book, in which those lives are set out for us, examples to imitate in whatever way we can as we seek to follow Jesus in the spirit of St Francis.

David Walker, Bishop of Manchester

Introduction

Being Christian and Franciscan

What does it mean to be a Franciscan? Is it someone who wears a brown robe and sandals; or someone inspired by the life of Saint Francis of Assisi? Is a Franciscan someone who is disturbed by the suffering of those who are poor, or by the perilous state of our planetary ecosystem; or simply someone who likes animals? Come to that, what does it mean to be a Christian? There are many ways to express our religious identity and probably most of the definitions we choose for ourselves will change fairly drastically at different stages of our lives. One of the ways of responding to these questions that makes most sense to me is the definition of being one who follows in the way of Francis of Assisi, or Jesus of Nazareth – becoming a companion of Francis and Jesus, or perhaps one who follows in their footsteps, even if it seems an audacious claim to make. And the means by which that commitment to follow in the way is articulated is to tell stories. Not in the sense of making things up, but in the sense of allowing the narratives of Christianity and the Franciscan tradition to be the framework around which I build my faith. The Franciscan tradition is deeply rooted in story-telling: stories about Francis of course, but also about his companions, such as Clare and Giles, later followers like Bonaventure and Angela of Foligno, and some of the slightly more obscure figures I will be talking about in this book. 'This is my story, this is my song,' goes the refrain of an old revivalist hymn, and this book is about discerning the song of the Franciscans in the first century after Francis, with the hope that in our own day we may learn the new song that Francis and his friends are teaching us today.

Perhaps it will help if in this introduction I sing some verses of my own song, not so much for the buzz of performance, but to suggest what instruments I bring to the symphony of the song of Francis and his companions. As Franciscans together practise and perform their parts in this symphony, it may become clearer what melodies and harmonies can be claimed as intrinsically Franciscan, and what may be discordant and best discarded, allowed to blow away on the wind.

There are many ways of becoming, or being, a Christian. I would say from my own experience that the Christian faith is more of a journey than an arrival. We are all on the way, like blind Bartimaeus of Jericho (Mark 10.52), and God gives us various companions as we journey on, helping us to keep our eyes on the destination far beyond us all. Indeed, the Acts of the Apostles describes Christians as followers of 'the Way' (Acts 24.14) and that seems to me to capture the mood of exploration, the stumbling and the getting up again, that so often characterize my tentative steps forward.

For me, a layer of my unfolding identity as a follower of Christ on the Way was my growing identity as a Franciscan. It began at Hilfield Friary in Dorset, now a sanctuary of ecological awareness, with a resident community of people dedicated to a sustainable life in harmony with the natural world. I spent three months many years ago living there as a volunteer, praying with the brothers in the chapel and digging the ground to make it ready for planting potatoes and other vegetables for the refectory table.

It was a brief but very significant time for me. It gave me a grounding in the Daily Office of prayer in the morning, at midday, in the early evening and at the close of day, where I could steep myself in the psalms and canticles, and the other Scripture readings. There was time for study too, and I enjoyed my encounters with some of the great saints of the Christian Church, such as the fourteenth-century English mystics Julian of Norwich, Richard Rolle and the anonymous writer of *The Cloud of Unknowing*. I also had the chance to read some of the stories and sayings of Francis of Assisi, being profoundly challenged by his commitment to a life of poverty, prayer and service of his fellow human beings.

Still, I felt that it was not yet time to commit myself to joining this community of Franciscans but chose instead to learn more about the religions of the world through inter-faith dialogue in England and later as a Church Mission Society mission partner in Korea. Meeting and making friends with missionary priests and sisters, as well as Buddhist monks and nuns, kept alive within me the inescapable question of whether this was the life to which I also was called. Eventually I ran out of excuses and returned to England to submit my application to join the Society of St Francis. From now on I would attempt to follow the footprints of Jesus in the company of St Francis and his followers through the ages.

Taking on the identity of a Franciscan friar was a new and exciting adventure. I arrived with no more than I could carry, having left behind my books and my savings account (which in any case was practically empty), and became a postulant of the Order, the first stage in a graduated process of progressive belonging. After four months I was 'clothed' as a novice and given the brown Franciscan habit to wear, including a hood, a pair of sandals and a single-knotted rope around my waist. Nick Worssam had become Brother Nicholas Alan SSF.

Outwardly, the change only took the time needed to sing five verses of a hymn, as I and my fellow novices rapidly changed out of our 'civilian' clothes and returned from the sacristy to the chapel in hastily adjusted habits, hoping not to trip over each other's clumsily tied trailing white ropes in the process. It was an emotional experience of homecoming, as though an identity that before had been slowly forming on the inside was now displayed on the outside for all to see. I have to say that it felt good.

So I had arrived, physically: I had become a Franciscan. But it took some time for the identity to seep into my bones. Becoming a Franciscan was easier than being a Franciscan to the core of my truest self. But gradually the outward symbols of the religious life worked their way into me and the stories of

Francis of Assisi and his companions became part of my own story.

In the current Church of England Common Worship service of Holy Baptism there is a helpful initial summary of the purpose of the rite:

> Our Lord Jesus Christ has told us that to enter the kingdom of heaven we must be born again of water and the Spirit, and has given us baptism as the sign and seal of this new birth. Here we are washed by the Holy Spirit and made clean. Here we are clothed with Christ, dying to sin that we may live his risen life. As children of God, we have a new dignity and God calls us to fullness of life.

In many ways this is a description of the journey of faith as a whole, which for me includes the commitment to a life in vows as a member of a religious community. The wearing of the habit is another means of entering the fellowship of the church, being 'clothed with Christ'; the rope tied around the waist is a symbol of being bound to Christ as he was bound to the cross, taking the yoke of obedience even to death and the new life beyond. The initial promise a novice makes to be obedient to the Rule and the brothers in positions of authority is widened out by the three-fold vow of poverty, chastity and obedience, a commitment made at what is known as our 'profession in vows'. First the vows are affirmed in a simple profession of faith in the calling of God to this life, then after some years of discernment, the vows are solemnly professed for the rest of our lives. These vows echo our baptismal vows and, with the invocation of the aid of the Holy Spirit, sign and seal us in our identity as a brother or sister in community, a companion of St Francis and a follower of the rabbi from Galilee whose baptism revealed him as God's beloved child.

Through this book I will be exploring ways in which the early companions and followers of Francis lived out their vocations to be new Franciscans in the world. They were all very different characters: inspiring, challenging, vexing and often mystifying as they tried to live this life with the greatest possible sincerity. There was no one way of being Franciscan, but together the stories and sayings here map out a territory for exploration, marking out where the paths are clearest and where there be dragons waiting to lure the unwitting traveller off the straight and narrow way. May they be a guide to your path and faithful companions on the way of your journey deeper into God.

I

The Founder: Francis of Assisi
(1182–1226)

This book is about what it means to be a Franciscan, a follower of the way of St Francis of Assisi, and gives examples of the many ways of doing this, encouraging each person to find some aspect in the life and teaching of the saint which particularly speaks to them. But what about Francis himself? Surely it was easy enough for him to be himself – what other option did he have? In fact, in the stories about him, we find many occasions when Francis is struggling against the opinions of others, with everyone telling him what he should do and be. Like any religious leader today, he had to live up to many hopes and expectations. In one of the compilations of stories about Francis, *A Mirror of the Perfection of a Lesser Brother*, there is an example of the exasperation Francis felt at being typecast in so many different ways:

When blessed Francis was at Saint Mary of the Portiuncula for the general chapter known as the Chapter of Mats because the only dwellings there were made of rush-mats, there were five thousand brothers present. Many wise and learned brothers went to the Lord of Ostia, who was there and told him: 'Lord, we want you to persuade Brother Francis to follow the advice of the wise brothers and allow himself to be guided by them.' They cited the *Rule* of blessed Benedict, blessed Augustine, and blessed Bernard, which teach how to live in such order in such a way.

The cardinal related everything to blessed Francis, giving him some advice as well. Then blessed Francis took him by the hand, saying nothing, and led him to the brothers assembled in chapter, and spoke to the brothers in the fervour and power of the Holy Spirit: 'My brothers! My brothers! God has called me by the way of simplicity and humility, and has truly shown me this way for me for those who want to trust and imitate me. Therefore I do not want you to mention to me any *Rule*, whether of Saint Augustine, or of Saint Bernard, or of Saint Benedict, or any other way or form of life except the one that the Lord in his mercy has shown and given to me. And the Lord told me what he wanted: he wanted me to be a new fool in this world. God did not wish to lead us by any way other than this knowledge, but God will confound you by your knowledge and wisdom.' The cardinal was greatly shocked, and said nothing, and all the brothers were greatly afraid. (*FA:ED*, vol. 3, pp. 313–14)

In relating this story, it is tempting to quietly edit away the last two sentences. This doesn't sound like the loveable friend of animals and children, the man who preached to the birds and sang with the crickets. But maybe Francis was a bit scarier than that and not immune from losing his temper from time to time. It may not be his best side, but this is more the raw personality that his first brothers both revered and sometimes feared. Here, Cardinal Hugolino, the Lord of Ostia, who was a Protector of the nascent Order and liaison with Pope Innocent III, is just trying to be helpful. He wants to get Francis to conform to the accepted patterns of religious life already established in the Church at the time, to ensure papal approval of the Order. Pope Innocent III had decreed that there should be no new orders, as he was concerned about the numbers of charismatic preachers wandering across Europe, all too easily making rival claims to spiritual authority and setting up their own distinctive communities. Somehow, Francis managed to slip under the net and have his Rule approved by the papacy, largely because of his great loyalty to the Church. Francis taught his brothers to defer to the priests and bishops in whose churches and dioceses they sought to share their message of peace, and a succession of popes saw the Franciscans as able to contain the fervour of the time, and able to harness it for the benefit of the Church as a whole.

At the end of his life Francis was still struggling to make his position clear. As he lay dying in the outskirts of Assisi, he wanted to leave one last summary of his life's work, his final *Testament*. He wanted to ensure that the legacy he had bequeathed to his brothers in the Order of Friars Minor, the 'Lesser Brothers', would be respected. Above all, he wanted the *Rule of 1223* and *The Testament* itself to be interpreted 'without gloss', that is, without adding or taking anything away from the words on the page. It was a last wish, but one that failed in its endeavour. Ironically, it was Pope Gregory IX, the former Cardinal Hugolino, who decided how the legacy of St Francis would be maintained and what it would mean for future generations to be Franciscan. In the papal decree of 1230 entitled *Quo Elongati*, Gregory instructed the Franciscan friars that, 'Wishing to remove all anxiety from your hearts, we declare that you are not bound by *The Testament*. For without the consent of the brothers, and especially of the ministers, Francis could not make obligatory a matter that touches everyone' (*FA:ED*, vol. 1, p. 571). Thus he declared that *The Testament* was a personal wish of Francis, without being legally binding. Nonetheless, *The Testament* gives a clear indication of the direction in which Francis wanted the Order to grow and is in many ways a summary of his life and mission. In this text Francis revealed the heart of his vocation, what he believed it meant to be Francis of Assisi:

And after the Lord gave me some brothers, no one showed me what I had to do, but the Most High Himself revealed to me that I should live according to the pattern of the Holy Gospel. And I had this written down simply and in a few words and the Lord Pope confirmed it for me. (*The Testament* 1226, *FA:ED*, vol. 1, p. 125)

What did it mean to be Francis, son of Pietro Bernardone, whom so many people now acclaimed as a saint? It was simply to live 'according to the pattern of the Holy Gospel'. But it is not so easy to articulate what this actually means. When Francis and his first companions went to Rome to ask for approval of their way of life, all they presented was a short list of gospel sayings. Pope Innocent was going to turn them away, saying that such a life seemed exceptionally hard and severe, but in the end the pope gave verbal approval to go and preach penance and to return to Rome when their life together had become more firmly established (*FA:ED*, vol. 2, p. 98).

As Francis and his brothers walked back to Assisi, their minds were still full of questions. They had been graciously received by Pope Innocent, but still they wondered:

> How could they carry out his advice and commands? How could they sincerely keep the rule they had accepted and steadfastly safeguard it? How could they walk before the Most High in all holiness and religion? Finally, how could their life and conduct, by growth in the holy virtues, be an example to their neighbours? (*FA:ED*, vol. 1, p. 213)

These were questions it would take them a lifetime to answer. But they had set out on their journey, they were on the road, and that seemed to be the place God wanted them to be.

A brother in arms

In fact, Francis had already travelled quite a distance along the road to holiness. As a rich young man, the son of a dealer in expensive cloth, Francis had spent his early years living a care-free and profligate life. Celano says in his *Life of St Francis*:

> He was an object of admiration to all, and he endeavoured to surpass others in his flamboyant display of vain accomplishments: wit, curiosity, practical jokes and foolish talk, songs, and soft and flowing garments. Since he was very rich, he was

not greedy but extravagant, not a hoarder of money but a squanderer of his property, a prudent dealer but a most unreliable steward. He was, nevertheless, a rather kindly person, adaptable and quite affable, even though it made him look foolish. (*FA:ED*, vol. 1, p. 183)

Francis, in his youth, seems to have been the life and soul of every party. He was universally popular, not least because he could afford to pay for a round of drinks to get the party going. All his life he liked to sing and the songs he chose were often those of the troubadours. These were travelling entertainers, wandering the byways of southern France and Italy, recounting deeds of valour and romance, such as the stories of King Arthur and the knights of the round table.

Francis himself longed to be a knight in shining armour. Perhaps he liked the thought of the camaraderie of war or dreamed of impressing the young ladies of Assisi by his chivalry and skill at arms. The chance came to put these dreams to the test in a battle between his home town of Assisi and the neighbouring town of Perugia. It was a conflict that had been simmering for several years during the first decade of the thirteenth century. It had been enflamed by the conflict in Assisi between the noble families (the *maiores*) and the popular class (the *minores*), which had led to the rich families of Assisi seeking refuge with their neighbours in Perugia. One skirmish in particular erupted in 1202 at Collestrada, in the area between the two warring towns. Francis fought alongside his fellow citizens but was captured and held in prison in Perugia until his family paid a ransom. Francis seemed to remain cheerful during this time, trying to lift the spirits of his fellow prisoners and keep them from venting their frustrations on each other, but it was necessarily a grim experience living in an overcrowded dungeon. Already, at a young age, Francis was learning the skills of peacemaking in the most difficult of circumstances.

After a year, Francis was freed and allowed to return to Assisi, but the experience of imprisonment had left him a broken man. Celano tells us that, worn down by illness,

Francis began to mull over within himself things that were not usual for him. When he had recovered a little and, with the support of a cane, had begun to walk about here and there through the house in order to regain his health, he went outside one day and began to gaze upon the surrounding countryside with greater interest. But the beauty of the fields, the delight of the vineyards, and whatever else was beautiful to see could offer him no delight at all. He wondered at the sudden change in himself, and considered those who loved these things quite foolish. (*FA:ED*, vol. 1, pp. 184–5)

As a sensitive young man, the experience of armed conflict and imprisonment had deeply affected Francis. Did he seriously injure, or even kill another man on the battlefield? Did he see friends of his, drinking companions from his nights of carousing, butchered by the swords and knives of his opponents? There is no way of knowing what his eyes saw and his ears heard, but the events of that day would have lodged themselves deeply in his memory. His illness could probably be classified as Post Traumatic Stress Disorder, as is experienced by so many in our own day, from ex-military personnel who have seen conflict at first hand, to nurses and doctors coping with the repeated witnessing of death in hospitals and care homes.

But still Francis had not fully learnt the lessons of war. A couple of years later, his physical strength renewed, Francis headed out once more to the battlefield, intent on becoming a true knight. He had heard that there was a conflict at Apulia in the south east of Italy and he wanted to become a brother in arms once more. Walter of Briene, in charge of the army of Pope Innocent III, was fighting against Markwald of Anweiler, representing the German Empire. Francis persuaded his father to provide him with all the best military equipment and rode off to battle hoping to be made a knight and so become a true member of the nobility. But it all came to nothing. First, he had a vision of a magnificent palace, the walls lined with weapons and the corridors filled with suits of armour. Thinking this to be a good omen before a battle, Francis hastened his preparations to look the part of a great soldier. But then, barely out of Assisi, he had another dream which undermined his martial resolve. In the dream he heard a voice saying, 'Who would you rather serve: a lord or his servant?' To which Francis replied, 'Lord, what do you want me to do?' On being told in the dream to return to Assisi, Francis changed his mind. He gave up his armour to a poor knight and went back into his home town to await further instructions.

The next mission he was to be given was not long in coming. Still in chivalrous mood, Francis roamed the deserted woods and dilapidated churches in the region of Assisi, searching for a way forward. One day in particular, he was praying in the run-down church of San Damiano, just outside the walls of Assisi. Kneeling before the crucifix hung from the ceiling of the sanctuary, he once more offered himself as a knight seeking a commission. It's as if he was asking for a trial to undergo, or a damsel in distress to rescue and bring safely home. But this time the lord he knelt in front of was not a soldier of this world, but the Lord who reigned from the cross. This was the prayer that Francis prayed before the crucifix:

> Most High, glorious God,
> enlighten the darkness of my heart
> and give me true faith, certain hope, and perfect charity,
> sense and knowledge, Lord,
> that I may carry out your holy and true command.
> (*FA:ED*, vol. 1, p. 40)

In response he heard a voice calling him by name, as the image of Christ crucified spoke to him, saying: 'Francis, go rebuild my house; as you see, it is all being destroyed' (*FA:ED*, vol. 2, p. 249). Being a literal-minded man, Francis began to physically rebuild the church in which he knelt, begging for building materials from the townspeople of Assisi. Maybe he had learnt some building skills in the dismantling of the castle at the top of the town, which had recently been sacked as part of the ongoing conflict between the rich and the poor in the town.

To raise money for this building project, Francis even went so far as to take a roll of cloth from his father's workshop and to ride with it to the nearby town of Foligno, where he sold both cloth and horse and offered the sum to the priest of the church at San Damiano. Hearing of this extravagance, Francis' father was enraged and brought him before the Bishop of Assisi, demanding the return of his property. In response, Francis made the extravagant gesture of not only returning the money, but even taking off his clothes before the crowd in Assisi as he threw them at the feet of his distraught father, saying, 'From now on I will say freely: "Our Father who art in heaven," and not "My father, Pietro di Bernardone"' (*FA:ED*, vol. 2, p. 251). It is a memorable scene, a grand gesture by someone eager to make a complete break with his past. Francis' journey continued, but from this point on his father disappears from the accounts of his life. Perhaps there was no possibility of a reconciliation, but it remains a sad fact that the man who dedicated his life to a message of forgiveness and peace was unable to be reconciled to his own father. Francis indeed prayed continually to his Father in heaven, as the prayers in his writings abundantly show, but, as far as we know, he was never able to pray again with his father on earth, the one who had nurtured, and in his own way, loved him all his life and who had no doubt hoped that Francis would take on the family business.

Francis now began to wear the clothing of a wandering hermit, complete with sandals, a staff and a tunic roughly marked with a cross, the symbol of the crusades. He was becoming a different kind of knight, a soldier in the army of the Lord.

Herald of the great King

It wasn't long before his fighting prowess was put to the test.

He who once enjoyed wearing scarlet robes now travelled about half-clothed. Once while he was singing praises to the

Lord in French in a certain forest, thieves suddenly attacked him. When they savagely demanded who he was, the man of God answered confidently and forcefully: 'I am the herald of the great King! What is it to you?' They beat him and threw him into a ditch filled with deep snow, saying: 'Lie there, you stupid herald of God!' After they left, he rolled about to and fro, shook the snow off himself and jumped out of the ditch. Exhilarated with great joy, he began in a loud voice to make the woods resound with praises to the Creator of all. (*FA:ED*, vol. I, p. 194)

Francis used to enjoy singing in French, a language he had probably picked up accompanying his merchant father on his journeys to trade fairs in France. Perhaps it was the troubadour songs that he sang to keep up his spirits. Even while begging for scraps of food, he would sometimes call out in French, so making a kind of game out of the humiliating experience of poverty and hunger. Even his name, Francis, was really a nickname, his baptismal name being John. Perhaps the name Francis was given to him by his friends as a kind of *nom de guerre* in their adolescent fights, or by his parents (his mother may herself have been born in France) as a term of endearment for their Francophile boy. His exuberance and sense of fun may not have endeared him to the bunch of thieves that he met in the snow, but it clearly helped him to maintain the carefree spirit that had been such a characteristic of his youth.

As 'the herald of the great King', what was his message to the world? What was the news that he was being commissioned to make known? Celano points to the centrality of the message of peace in the preaching of St Francis:

In all of his preaching, before he presented the word of God to the assembly, [Francis] prayed for peace saying, 'May the Lord give you peace.' He always proclaimed this to men and women, to those he met and to those who met him. Accordingly, many who hated peace along with salvation, with the Lord's help wholeheartedly embraced peace. They became

14

themselves children of peace, now rivals for eternal salvation. (*FA:ED*, vol. 1, p. 203)

Of course, Francis was not alone in preaching this message. He even seems to have had a direct predecessor to his mission who used the slogan: 'Peace and good! Peace and good!' It is not known who this was who went through Assisi announcing this greeting, or whether Francis used the same phrase himself (the text in *The Legend of the Three Companions* (*FA:ED*, vol. 2, p. 84) is not clear). Nonetheless, the phrase in its Latin form, *pax et bonum*, or in modern Italian, *pace e bene*, has since become a motto of the Franciscan tradition, gracing many a communal letterhead, logo or email greeting.

The phrase itself is slightly awkward in Latin, but it echoes a passage from the prophet Isaiah: 'How beautiful upon the mountains are the feet of the messenger who announces peace, who brings good news, who announces salvation, who says to Zion, "Your God reigns"' (Isa. 52.7), and this may have been the source of Francis' inspiration. The greeting of peace is in any case a universal greeting in the Holy Land, using the word *shalom* (in Hebrew) or *salaam* (in Arabic). It was used by Jesus in his instructions to the first disciples, as he taught them, 'Whatever house you enter, first say, "Peace to this house!"' (Luke 10.5). St Peter greets the household of Cornelius in a similar way, saying: 'You know the message [God] sent to the people of Israel, preaching peace by Jesus Christ – he is Lord of all' (Acts 10.36). St Paul echoes this as he rounds off his Second Letter to the Thessalonians (3.16): 'Now may the Lord of peace himself give you peace at all times in all ways.' Francis commends this greeting in *The Testament*, and in *The Admonitions* he praises those who work for peace:

'Blessed are the peacemakers, for they will be called children of God.' (Matt. 5.9)
Those people are truly peacemakers who, regardless of what they suffer in this world, preserve peace of spirit and body out of love of our Lord Jesus Christ. (*FA:ED*, vol. 1, p. 134)

For Francis, the greeting of peace was not just a mere formality. It had to emerge from a heart full of peace. And peace with others was rooted in the love of Jesus Christ, which is why he spent so much time in prayer. He was searching for the inward reconciliation with God that would enable him to be an outward reconciler of people, regardless of the difficulties of the situation. As he says in another of the *Admonitions*, also based on the same verse from Matthew's Gospel, under the title 'Patience':

> A servant of God cannot know how much patience and humility he has within himself as long as he is content. When the time comes, however, when those who should make him content do the opposite, he has as much patience and humility as he has at that time and no more. (*FA:ED*, vol. 1, p. 133)

The work of reconciliation is not a time for self-deception. Rather, it is in the experience of opposition that the hidden treasures of patience and humility can be most readily found. In one of the most complete of *The Admonitions*, Francis mapped out the values that undergirded his whole life as a messenger of peace:

> [1] Where there is charity and wisdom,
> there is neither fear nor ignorance.
> [2] Where there is patience and humility,
> there is neither anger nor disturbance.
> [3] Where there is poverty with joy,
> there is neither greed nor avarice.
> [4] Where there is rest and meditation,
> there is neither anxiety nor restlessness.
> [5] Where there is fear of the Lord to guard an entrance,
> there the enemy cannot have a place to enter.
> [6] Where there is a heart full of mercy and discernment,
> there is neither excess nor hardness of heart.
> *Admonition* 27 (*FA:ED*, vol. 1, pp. 136–7)

This was the manifesto of Francis, his plan of campaign. It is a passage worth meditating on at length – how love drives out fear and wisdom overcomes ignorance; how patience is the antidote to anger and how humility calms disturbance. Above all, for Francis, the life of peacemaking is rooted in the valuing of poverty with joy: not poverty as a grim deprivation, but the glad relinquishing of all that separates people from each other. The cultivation of these qualities is based on rest and medi-tation, seeking to be alone with the Lord and pondering deeply the words of Scripture. Knowing the fear of the Lord is the beginning of wisdom, according to the Book of Proverbs; there is also knowing the fear that the Father himself experiences as he trembles with solicitude for his Son and all his children. Finally, when the heart is full of mercy, situations of conflict can be steered towards a just resolution and forgiveness for all can be found.

Brothers in alms

In his search for clarity as to how to serve his Lord in the world, Francis spent long hours in solitary prayer. He found a cave near Assisi, no one knows exactly where, to which he would retreat to give himself time for contemplative prayer. Even then he was not completely alone, as a close friend would go with him, and make sure that no one disturbed his silence and solitude. Francis said afterwards that he found a great treasure in that hidden place – perhaps the treasure of the gospel, or a revelation of the love of God his Father.

But still Francis wanted to know how to spend the days God had given him, now that he was no longer a businessman tied to making a profit in the cloth trade. The answer was not long in coming, as described in *The Legend of the Three Com-panions*:

Then, one day at Mass, he heard those things which Christ tells the disciples who were sent out to preach, instructing them to carry no gold or silver or a wallet or purse, bread, walking stick, or shoes, or two tunics. After understanding this more clearly because of the priest, he was filled with indescribable joy. 'This,' he said, 'is what I want to do with all my strength.' And so, after committing to memory everything he had heard, he joyfully fulfilled them, removing his second garment without delay, and from then on never used a walking stick, shoes, purse, or wallet. He made for himself a very cheap and plain tunic, and, throwing the belt away, he girded himself with a cord. (*FA:ED*, vol. 2, p. 84)

The day was the feast of St Matthias, commemorated on 24 February in the time of Francis, and the Gospel reading was most likely Matthew 10.9–10, as related above. It gave him the commission he had been longing for: the 'pattern of the holy Gospel' as he phrased it in his *Testament*. But still he wanted to make sure that he had got it right and the opportunity to test his understanding soon arose.

Not long after this, Francis was joined by his first companions, Bernard and Peter. Bernard of Quintavalle was a rich man of Assisi and he wanted to know what to do with his many possessions, if indeed he was to join Francis in his life of prayer and simple preaching of the gospel. The only place they knew to search for guidance was the Bible, so they went to the church of San Nicolo in Assisi to consult the Word of God. There they placed the book of the Gospels reverently on the altar, made the sign of the cross and prayed that God would make his will clear. Opening the book at random, the first passage they found was the counsel of Jesus, saying: 'If you wish to be perfect, go, sell your possessions, and give the money to the poor, and you will have treasure in heaven; then come, follow me' (Matt. 19.21). The opening of the Bible at random, while not considered such a helpful method of Bible study today, was a common and accepted practice at the time of Francis. So they tried again, twice more, just to be certain, and to honour the Holy Trinity. The second time they opened the book they saw the same passage that had already inspired Francis, from

Matthew 10, about taking nothing for the journey. Finally, they opened the book of the Gospels a third time and read the unmistakable instruction: 'If any want to become my followers, let them deny themselves and take up their cross and follow me' (Matt. 16.24). Rejoicing in this divine confirmation, Francis cried out: 'Brothers, this is our life and rule and that of all who will want to join our company. Go, therefore, and fulfil what you have heard' (*FA:ED*, vol. 2, p. 86). Thomas of Celano concludes his version of the story with a return to martial imagery:

> Francis, filled with the spirit of God, then understood that he would have to enter into the kingdom of God through many trials, difficulties and struggles. The brave soldier was not disturbed by oncoming battles, nor was he downcast in his spirit as he was about to fight the wars of the Lord in the camps of this world. (*FA:ED*, vol. 1, p. 263)

Beginning to do penance

In his desire to be a soldier who brings peace, Francis taught his brothers to live a life of penance, that is, living a life dedicated to the reconciliation of people with each other, and of everyone with God. Penance included penitence, sorrow for one's sins and the desire to set things right with God and one's neighbour, but was also a much wider term that embraced a whole lifestyle of wanting to be an agent of reconciliation. As Celano put it:

> In his desire for holiness he was simple with the simple, humble with the humble, and poor with the poor. He was a brother among brothers, the least among the lesser, and in his life and habits strove to behave as one of them as much as was possible ... [Francis] led the strangers back to the way, made peace between those in conflict, and bound together those in peace in a stronger bond of love. (*FA:ED*, vol. 1, p. 269)

One of the ways that was dearest to him, which he recalled at the beginning of his *Testament*, was that of humble service to others, especially those suffering from leprosy, which was particularly prevalent at the time of Francis. These were the real outcasts of medieval society, compelled to live away from the towns in 'hospitals' where they received minimal care and of which there were at least three in the vicinity of Assisi at that time. If they dared come near inhabited areas, they had to ring a bell to announce their presence, so that others could avoid them and so reduce the risk of being infected by what was believed to be an incurable disease. Francis was typical of his day, experiencing a horror of the disfigurement and smell the condition entailed. But then one day, that all changed when he forced himself to go and greet a man with leprosy, and in so doing overcame his abhorrence and fear.

> The Lord gave me, Brother Francis, thus to begin doing penance in this way: for when I was in sin, it seemed too bitter for me to see lepers. And the Lord Himself led me among them and I showed mercy to them. And when I left them, what had seemed bitter to me was turned into sweetness of soul and body. And afterwards I delayed a little and left the world. (*The Testament, FA:ED*, vol. 1, p. 124)

Penance, for Francis, was not solely a personal religious devotion to be practised behind closed doors. He did indeed pray for long hours in solitary locations; but he also needed to put his prayers into action, in this case leading him to care for the people with leprosy, who had before been a bitter sight to his eyes. This was all part of his conversion experience: embracing the shadow side of life, seeing in sickness the opportunity to practise humility and compassion. It didn't take him long to realize that this was all part of a project that would take all the energy he had. Not that he would always be a nurse in the strict sense, but that the delights of the world would now be a distraction for him and that he would have to 'leave the world', that is, enter a religious community, if he was going to be able to serve God and his neighbour with the rigour to which he felt called. This was not an escape but an enchantment, a finding of delight in the service of others. It was not the only way of living a life of service: for those with marital and family commitments there were plenty of opportunities for self-sacrificial, loving service of others. Francis recognized this when he founded the Third Order later in his ministry, in which people, married or single, could fully express their devotion to the Lord without taking a vow of celibacy in the First Order of Brothers or the Second Order of Sisters. Francis himself was torn between the two ways of life – community and family – and struggled to know which was best for him (see *FA:ED*, vol. 2, pp. 324–5), but in the end he chose Lady Poverty to be his life-long companion and friend. Yet even that commitment to a celibate life he had to constantly reaffirm – 'Often, when many were calling him blessed, he would reply with these words: "Don't praise me as if I were safe; I can still have sons and daughters!"' (*FA:ED*, vol. 2, p. 333).

Going into the heart of the enemy

Like many people in his day, Francis longed to visit the Holy Land, to walk in the same places where Jesus had walked, and to spend time in prayer at the shrines commemorating his Passion and death. He also encouraged his brothers to go to the lands of the 'Saracens', that is, the Muslims. In his *Earlier Rule* of 1221 Francis described two possible ways of going on such a missionary expedition:

As for the brothers who go, they can live spiritually among the Saracens and nonbelievers in two ways. One way is not to engage in arguments or disputes but to be subject to every human creature for God's sake and to acknowledge that they are Christians. The other way is to announce the Word of God, when they see it pleases the Lord, in order that [unbelievers] may believe in almighty God, the Father, the Son and the Holy Spirit ...

Wherever they may be, let all my brothers remember that they have given themselves and abandoned their bodies to the Lord Jesus Christ. For love of him, they must make themselves vulnerable to their enemies, both visible and invisible. (*FA:ED*, vol. i, p. 74)

This is a remarkable passage because it goes against the popular practice of going to Muslim countries with the express wish of being martyred for the faith and so going straight to heaven. Instead, Francis offers the option of simply being present, acknowledging their faith if asked, but not provoking a violent confrontation. The brothers were to 'make themselves vulnerable to their enemies, both visible and invisible'. This non-violent approach to mission encompassed even their invisible enemies – the demons – who would presumably be disarmed by such humility, just as Jesus made himself vulnerable on the cross and won the salvation of the world.

The opportunity came for Francis to put these counsels into effect in his own life. During the height of the fifth Crusade, while a Christian army was besieging Damietta in Egypt, Francis travelled by boat to join the Christian camp. Rather than enlist as a soldier, Francis and a companion named Illuminato walked straight into no man's land between the two armies and asked to be taken to the Sultan Malik al-Kamil. Remarkably, the two friars were taken through the ranks of soldiers and presented to the sultan himself. There they engaged in a dialogue about the true faith and the sultan was so impressed that he gave Francis free passage through the Holy Land on his way back to Italy. Of course, Francis would have been delighted if the sultan had become a Christian – that would, after all, have meant the end of the crusade and the departure of the Christian armies in peace. It may even be that Francis kept an ongoing concern for the salvation of the sultan, praying for him especially during his retreat on Mount La Verna.

At least, this is the story from the perspective of the Latin sources. Scholars have been perplexed by the fact that there is no record of this meeting between Francis and the sultan in any Arabic texts of the time. This may be because what for Francis and his companion was a deeply significant meeting, which they recounted to others on their return, may have been for the sultan and his entourage a barely memorable chance encounter. Dialogue is by nature a two-way conversation, and it would be fascinating to discover what the sultan really thought about this Christian holy man, in many ways so like the sufis of Islam.

But what is striking about the story, at least from the Christian point of view, is the insistence by Francis that the threat of war could only be overcome by dialogue and by making oneself vulnerable to one's enemies. In fact, for Francis, there were no true enemies, but all people, all creatures, were his brothers and sisters, his blood relations, as we will see when examining his 'Canticle of the Creatures'.

Preaching to the birds

Francis didn't only preach to humans, he also, famously, preached to a flock of birds. It happened one day when he was travelling through the Spoleto valley. When he and his companions came close to the birds, Francis ran towards them and gave his usual greeting 'The Lord give you peace!' Surprisingly, the birds didn't fly away, but allowed Francis to walk among them, touching their heads and bodies with his tunic and exhorting them to praise and love God, who provided all that they needed. Celano completes the story:

> After the birds had listened so reverently to the word of God, he began to accuse himself of negligence because he had not preached to them before. From that day on, he carefully exhorted all birds, all animals, all reptiles, and also insensible creatures, to praise and love the Creator, because

daily, invoking the name of the Saviour, he observed their obedience in his own experience. (*FA:ED*, vol. 1, p. 234)

Why did Francis preach to the birds? In many of the stories about Francis befriending animals, there is a delightful sense of him simply overflowing with joy. Francis lived in a diaphanous world: he could see through everything as if it were just a window onto eternity. Everything spoke to him of the presence of God. He had an acute sense of the ceaseless praise to God offered by all creatures simply by being what they were, displaying an obedience to the will of God in their very being. Francis chided himself because he had not previously included the creatures in his prayers in a fully conscious way. Now he saw more clearly that all that lives is somehow holy; all creatures thrive because God loves them and provides for them, and humanity should likewise include all that lives in its compassionate stewardship of the earth.

Francis humanized creation, treating animals as companions in the spiritual life, colleagues and servants of God's kingdom. On beginning a retreat at La Verna, the chirping birds flying around the hermitage seemed to him to be issuing a personal welcome and an encouragement to pray. Another time the singing of birds caused Francis to get out his prayer book and sing the Office with them, at least until the birds began to sing too loudly and he asked them to stop for a while so that he and his brothers could sing their part (*FA:ED*, vol. 2, pp. 592–3). In this way he was enacting the Scriptures, particularly passages such as The Song of the Three (The Prayer of Azariah) and Psalm 148, both of which exhort all the earth to praise the Lord.

Francis was steeped in the psalms and Psalm 104 seems to have spoken to him in a special way:

O Lord, how manifold are your works!
In wisdom you have made them all;
the earth is full of your creatures ...
These all look to you
to give them their food in due season;

when you give to them, they gather it up;
when you open your hand, they are filled with good things.
(Ps. 104.24, 27–28)

The preaching to the birds is just one of many stories about
Francis befriending animals, or being moved by their sufferings. Francis felt an affectionate compassion for all living
creatures, particularly those who reminded him of his Lord,
such as lambs being taken to market, reminding him of Jesus
the Lamb of God slaughtered for the salvation of the world.
The classic expression of Francis' attitude to creation is seen
in his 'Canticle of the Creatures', written at a time of great
sickness and pain, just two years before his death, when he was
suffering from an eye disease that left him unable to endure
sunlight. He wrote it as a hymn of creation, an exhortation to
all things to join in the praise of God, together with the angels
and saints. The canticle begins:

¹ Most High, all-powerful, good Lord,
Yours are the praises, the glory, and the honour, and
    all blessing,
² To You alone, Most High, do they belong,
and no human is worthy to mention Your name.
³ Praised be You, my Lord, with all Your creatures,
especially Sir Brother Sun,
Who is the day and through whom You give us light.
⁴ And he is beautiful and radiant with great splendour;
and bears a likeness of You, Most High One.
⁵ Praised be You, my Lord, through Sister Moon and
    the stars,
in heaven You formed them clear and precious and beautiful.
⁶ Praised be You, my Lord, through Brother Wind,
and through the air, cloudy and serene, and every kind
    of weather,
through whom You give sustenance to Your creatures.
⁷ Praised be You, my Lord, through Sister Water,
who is very useful and humble and precious and chaste.

[8] Praised be You, my Lord, through Brother Fire,
through whom You light the night,
and he is beautiful and playful and robust and strong.
[9] Praised be You, my Lord, through our Sister Mother Earth,
who sustains and governs us,
and who produces various fruit with coloured flowers
   and herbs.
(*FA:ED*, vol. 1, pp. 113–14)

Surprisingly, although this is a song about creatures, no animals or birds are actually mentioned, and even humans are not represented in this first part of the song. It could be that this is because the canticle is not only a hymn of praise; it also has a hint of lament. In the second stanza, Francis says of the Most High that 'no human is worthy to mention your name', so he begins with 'Sir Brother Sun', who 'is beautiful and radiant with great splendour' and 'bears a likeness' to the Most High. Indeed Francis refers to the song as the 'Canticle of Brother Sun' (*FA:ED*, vol. 3, p. 367). Francis then goes a step further and sings of the interconnectedness of the whole universe, including the moon and the stars, which together with the sun he would have seen in his medieval world view as having a kind of consciousness of their own. The stars were seen as angelic beings, praising God and rejoicing at the creation of the world (see Psalm 19). Even the elements themselves, the air, the water, the fire and the earth, that together form the structures of existence, are part of this kaleidoscope of praise. Such worship unites all things in harmony. God is praised through, with, by and for all of creation, the Italian preposition *per* bearing all these possible meanings.

At this point, Francis composed a melody for the canticle and taught it to his brothers, but the song wasn't yet complete. Francis heard of a dispute between the mayor and the Bishop of Assisi, so he added an extra verse and told two of his brothers to serenade the feuding parties until they saw sense and were reconciled. There is hope for humanity: people can join in with the hymn of the universe, as Teilhard de Chardin called it, as long as they forgive each other and live in peace.

¹⁰ Praised be You, my Lord, through those who give pardon
   for Your love,
and bear infirmity and tribulation.
¹¹ Blessed are those who endure in peace
for by You, Most High, shall they be crowned.
(*FA:ED*, vol. 1, p. 114)

Finally, there is the last reconciliation, with Sister Death. Francis welcomed her with open arms not long after writing and reciting this last stanza of his song.

¹² Praised be You, my Lord, through our Sister Bodily Death,
from whom no one living can escape.
¹³ Woe to those who die in mortal sin.
Blessed are those whom death will find in Your most holy will,
for the second death shall do them no harm.
¹⁴ Praise and bless my Lord and give Him thanks
and serve Him with great humility.
(*FA:ED*, vol. 1, p. 114)

Fear of death and the subsequent judgement by God was ubiquitous in medieval religion and Francis was no exception. To die in mortal sin meant to die without having confessed a sin that led inevitably to the realms of judgement, so graphically described by Dante in his *Divine Comedy* written in the fourteenth century. The 'second death' that Francis mentions is that described in the Book of Revelation (20.14), the 'lake of fire'. We may not use terms like this in the modern world, but for medieval people, the fear of hell was an ever-present source of anxiety, fuelled by paintings in churches depicting the Last Judgement. Nonetheless, the song of St Francis ends on a high note, recalling the hearer to praise, blessing and the love and humility that drive out fear.

Francis began his search for a vocation with what seemed to him to be a call to arms. As it unfolded, his life became one of disarmament and the discovery that all things are our brothers and sisters. All of creation is a divine choir singing the praises of God, whether or not it can conceive of God's reality. One of the keys that opens the door to the inter-related universe of God's love is the experience of poverty – not as a rejection of the good things that God has given us, but as a celebration of all that can be held in common and enjoyed by all.

On one occasion, Francis and the Bishop of Assisi had a debate about the meaning of poverty:

> Lord, [said Francis] if we had possessions, we would need arms for our protection. For disputes and lawsuits usually arise out of them, and, because of this, love of God and neighbour are greatly impeded. Therefore, we do not want to possess anything in this world. (*FA:ED*, vol. 2, p. 89)

For Francis, giving up everything meant receiving sustenance from all things – the sun and the moon, the rain and the wind, our sister Mother Earth who nurtures us day by day. It meant being reconciled to one's enemies, choosing always the way of non-violent reconciliation, never the way of bloody confronta-tion. It meant not holding on even to life itself, but welcoming Sister Death, the friend of our final moment. And at the last, it meant trusting God in his compassion to bring us through the last letting go, to be with his saints for ever.

Brother John the Simple

Thomas of Celano, his first biographer, recorded one of Fran-cis' last instructions to his brothers: 'Let us begin, brothers, to serve the Lord God, for up until now we have done little or nothing' (*FA:ED*, vol. 1, p. 273). In this chapter we have looked at some of the ways Francis managed to discover him-self and his mission through the lens of his devotion to peace and reconciliation. This is a hugely important message in our own day, with so much dialogue in the public sphere being divisive and derisive, not so much dialogue as diatribe against those whom we consider different from ourselves. Francis is a great role model in undermining the practice of exclusion in our own day. But that doesn't mean that we should live out the universal virtues of humility and patience in exactly the same way. Francis said to his brothers at the end of his life: 'I have done what was given to me by the Lord; now it is for you to find what you should do' (see *FA:ED*, vol. 2, p. 386).

Lest we get too attached to the infinitely compelling poor man of Assisi, I end this chapter with the cautionary tale of Brother John the Simple. (Look out for the twist in the tale. Is the imitator really to be imitated?)

Once, when Saint Francis was passing by a village near Assisi, a certain John, a very simple man, was ploughing in the field. He ran to him, saying: 'I want you to make me a brother, for a long time now I have wanted to serve God.' The saint rejoiced noticing the man's simplicity, and responded to his intention: 'Brother, if you want to be our companion, give to the poor if you have anything, and once rid of your property, I will receive you.' He immediately unyoked the oxen and offered one to Saint Francis saying: 'Let's give this ox to the poor! I am sure I deserve to get this much as my share of my father's things.' The saint smiled, but he heartily approved his sense of simplicity. Now, when the parents and younger brothers heard of this, they hurried over in tears, grieving more over losing the ox than the man. The saint said to them: 'Calm down! Here, I'll give you back the ox and only take away the brother.' And so he took the man with him, and, dressed in the clothing of the Order, he made him his special companion because of his gift of simplicity.

Whenever Saint Francis stayed in some place to meditate, simple John would immediately repeat and copy whatever gestures or movements the saint made. If he spat, John would spit too, if he coughed, he would cough as well, sighing or sobbing along with him. If the saint lifted up his hands to heaven, John would raise his too, and he watched him intently as a model, turning himself into a copy of all his actions. The saint noticed this, and once asked him why he did those things. He replied: 'I promised to do everything you do. It is dangerous for me to leave anything out.' The saint delighted in this pure simplicity, but gently told him not to do this anymore. Shortly after this the simple man departed to the Lord in this same purity. The saint often proposed his life as worth imitating and merrily calling him not Brother John, but Saint John. (*FA:ED*, vol. 2, pp. 368–9)

2

The Companion: Clare of Assisi
(1194–1253)

Foundations

The Order of St Clare, the second of the three orders founded
by St Francis of Assisi, was first conceived on a building site.
Francis was busily repairing the church of San Damiano just
outside the walls of Assisi, when he was overcome by a sudden
inspiration. Clare proudly wrote about this in her *Testament*,
as she retold for her sisters the story of their foundation:

> The holy man [Francis] made a prophecy about us that the
> Lord later fulfilled. Climbing the wall of that church, he
> shouted in French to some poor people who were standing
> nearby: 'Come and help me in the work on the monastery
> of San Damiano, because there will as yet be ladies here
> who will glorify our heavenly Father throughout his holy,
> universal Church by their celebrated and holy manner of
> life.' We can consider in this, therefore, the abundant kind-
> ness of God to us. Because of his mercy and love, he saw fit to
> speak these words about our vocation and election through
> his saint. (*CA:ED*, pp. 60–1)

In the previous chapter, we looked at the progressive conversion of Francis, how he was gradually able to piece together
the principles by which he felt called to live. One of the significant crossroads of that journey was encountered when he was
praying in the dilapidated church of San Damiano and heard
the voice of Jesus calling to him from the crucifix, telling him to

rebuild the church which was falling into ruins. Francis eagerly embraced this new vocation of builder's labourer, begging for stones and mortar and hoisting them up the crumbling walls. That he prophesied about the holy ladies in French may well have mystified the poor people listening to his shout, but that was all part of the fun for Francis. He had seen a vision of the future and was eagerly bringing it into being; he was building a home for the Lord and for his sisters.

Francis wasn't the only one having visions. Pope Innocent III had dreamt about another ecclesiastical building. He had seen a little poor man holding up the cathedral church of St John Lateran in Rome, as if balancing the huge edifice as it rested on his shoulder. When they met, the pope recognized Francis as the man of his vision and gave him approval to dedicate himself to the rebuilding of the whole Church. In this way, the hod-carrier became the bearer of the gospel; the labourer repairing the walls of God's sanctuary became a surgeon of souls.

The Lord gave me Sisters

In his own *Testament*, Francis remembered the time God gave him brothers to share in his calling to renew the Church by preaching and praying for peace. But he was given sisters too, chief and first among them being the Lady Clare, daughter of the nobleman Favarone di Offreducio and his wife Ortolana. In Clare's *Testament*, she celebrates with overflowing gratitude the blessings of her vocation, speaking of the call to a life of penance, that is of poverty, prayer, silence and fasting, as being the expression of God's kindness to her and her sisters. All of it was rooted in the prophecy of Francis, the Holy Spirit speaking through him concerning a vocation that Clare herself had not yet begun to live. Although he had no brothers to share his life as yet, it is possible that Francis already knew Clare and that a friendship had begun to blossom between them, even if at a distance.

Clare was born in 1193 or 1194 and lived in a grand house in the centre of Assisi, next to the Cathedral of San Rufino. It may well be that she heard Francis preaching in the cathedral or in the market place below her window. In any case, she would have heard the gossip about the rich young trader's son, who had 'left the world' by abandoning home and family, setting out on a life of poverty, prayer and ministry to the sick. The two young people contrived to meet each other, with a trusted chaperone, to talk about their understanding of the gospel. Gradually, Clare came to realize that her life's calling was to be alongside Francis in his abandonment to the providence of God.

The day of her flight from the ties of family and society came on Palm Sunday 1212, when she was about 21 years old and Francis was in his early 30s. Attending church as usual, Clare did not join the procession to receive a palm cross together with the other members of her household, but instead the bishop came to her to give her his blessing. Was this a sign between the two of them that this was to be the day of her escape? That night, together with a companion, Clare crept out of the family house and left Assisi, perhaps by the Moiano gate, an entrance controlled by the bishop. From there she hurried down the hill to the tiny church of St Mary of the Angels, where Francis and his brothers were waiting to receive her. Removing her veil and letting her hair fall onto her shoulders, Clare offered herself to receive the monastic tonsure, the cutting of her hair as a sign of her dedication to God in the religious life.

Realizing that she could not avoid scandal if she stayed any longer with Francis and the brothers, Clare went first to stay at the Benedictine monastery of San Paolo, just a short distance away. There she would be safe from the members of her family who would no doubt want to reclaim their daughter for a marriage alliance to strengthen the clan's place in society. As expected, her uncle and brothers came to the monastery as soon as they discovered her absence, but Clare clung to the altar in the monastery chapel, showing them her shaved head as a witness to her resolve. Enraged, they nevertheless accepted

Clare's declaration of intent and the sanctuary of the holy place was left intact.

In her *Testament*, Clare continues to reminisce with her sisters, telling the story of how the filaments of her life were interwoven with those of Francis and his companions:

> After the most high heavenly Father saw fit in mercy and grace to enlighten my heart that I might do penance according to the example and teaching of our most blessed father Francis, a short while after his conversion, I, together with a few sisters whom the Lord had given me after my own conversion, willingly promised him obedience, as the Lord gave us the light of his grace through his wonderful life and teaching. When the blessed Francis saw, however, that, although we were physically weak and frail, we did not shirk deprivation, poverty, hard work, trial, or the shame or contempt of the world – rather, we considered them as great delights, as he had frequently examined us according to the example of the saints and his brothers – he greatly rejoiced in the Lord. And moved by pity for us, he bound himself, both personally and through his religion, always to have the same loving care and special solicitude for us as for his own brothers. (*CA:ED*, p. 61)

Francis and Clare were bound to each other – she to him by obedience, love and admiration, together with hard work and a life-long dedication to poverty, and he to her by loving care and the example of his life and teaching. Shortly after her escape to the Benedictine nuns at San Paolo, Clare moved on to the small community of women at Sant' Angelo in Panzo. This was probably not a strict monastic establishment but a gathering of holy women, committed to a life of prayer and manual labour: supporting themselves, and those too poor to fend for themselves, with their handiwork. There her blood sister Catherine came to join Clare, taking the name Sister Agnes. Again, the family reacted with great hostility and came to literally drag Agnes back to the family home. Clare could do nothing but pray desperately for help, which came by miraculous means. Suddenly the pursuers lost their strength, or at least their resolve, and found themselves unable to commit the violent act they had intended. Leaving the sisters behind, they stormed off, no doubt with much cursing, wondering what on earth had got into these normally docile, obedient young women. Perhaps this was what Clare was referring to in her *Testament* as 'the shame or contempt of the world' that they had faced together and overcome.

The riches of poverty

After these events, there was just one more move for Clare and her growing band of sisters: their relocation to the Church of San Damiano, which was to be their home for the rest of their lives. Once settled in this place, Francis laid out for the sisters his vision for their life, and his encouragement to them to love holy poverty above all things:

> Afterwards he wrote a form of life for us, especially that we would always persevere in holy poverty. While he was living he was not content to encourage us with many words and examples to the love of holy poverty and its observance, but he gave us many writings that, after his death, we would in no way turn away from it, as the Son of God never wished to turn away from this holy poverty while he lived in the world. And, while he lived, our most blessed father Francis, having imitated his footprints, never either in example or in teaching turned away from this holy poverty that he had chosen for himself and his brothers. (*CA:ED*, pp. 61–2)

This desire to live in holy poverty became one of the central pillars of the community gathered with Clare just outside Assisi, and of the other monasteries later affiliated to the Poor Ladies of San Damiano. In fact, Clare talks more about poverty than Francis does in his own writings. This was the strongest link between them, the source of their mutual blessing in the Son of God. Both of them would quote in their writings the passage of St Paul: 'For you know the generous act of our Lord Jesus Christ, that though he was rich, yet for your sakes he became poor, so that by his poverty you might become rich' (2 Cor. 8.9).

Freely chosen poverty, rather than the grinding, dehumanizing poverty imposed on the destitute in society, was a basic virtue for both Francis and Clare. It enfleshed two central theological themes in the teaching of the Church – the incarnation and the Passion of Jesus Christ, the Son of God. Devotion to the incarnate Son in his embrace of poverty was enacted and popularized by Francis in his establishment of the Christmas crib at Greccio, a tableau so realistic that the baby in the manger seemed to be a real, gurgling child. In her 'First Letter to Agnes of Prague', Clare wrote of her own understanding of holy poverty, which she, like Francis, described as Lady Poverty, 'who bestows eternal riches on those who love and embrace her!'

O God-centred poverty,
whom the Lord Jesus Christ
who ruled and still rules heaven and earth,
who spoke and things were made,
came down to embrace before all else!
He says: For the foxes have dens, and the birds of the air have nests, but the Son of Man, Christ, has nowhere to lay his head, but bowing his head he gave up his spirit.
If so great and good a Lord, then, on coming into the Virgin's womb, wanted to appear despised, needy, and poor in this world, so that people who were very poor and needy, suffering excessive hunger of heavenly nourishment, may become rich in him by possessing the kingdom of heaven, be very joyful and glad, filled with a remarkable happiness and a spiritual joy! (*CA:ED*, p. 45)

This is 'God-centred poverty' (Latin: *pia paupertas*; literally 'pious poverty'), freely embraced out of love and joy. It is the poverty of the homeless Jesus, the Son of Man, the poverty of the one who gave up even his life for the salvation of the world. The Franciscans called this 'the Sacred Exchange' ('*Sacrum Commercium*'), which was the title of an early allegorical story of Francis and his search for Lady Poverty. It was a kind of 'holy deal', in which by his incarnation the Son of God exchanged his riches for our poverty, that humanity might exchange its poverty for a share in the riches of Christ's divinity.

This desire for the riches of poverty was spoken about by the Franciscans using the literary form of the language of courtesy and romance. In this way, both Francis and Clare drew from the prevailing cultural background of courtly love, baptizing it with Christian imagery to make Lady Poverty a chaste beauty who could only be embraced by a chaste love.

In *The Form of Life of St Clare*, the monastic rule that Clare wrote for herself and her sisters, the central and most personal chapter (chapter 6) recounts the blessing of Francis, and Clare's response:

'I, little brother Francis, wish to follow the life and poverty of our most high Lord Jesus Christ and of his most holy Mother and to persevere in this until the end; and I ask you, my ladies, and I give you my advice that you live always in this most holy life and poverty. And keep careful watch that you never depart from this by reason of the teaching or advice of anyone.'

As I, [Clare] together with my sisters, have ever been solicitous to safeguard the holy poverty which we have promised the Lord God and blessed Francis, so, too, the abbesses who shall succeed me in office and all the sisters are bound inviolably to observe it to the end, that is, by not receiving or having possession or ownership either of themselves or through an intermediary, or even anything that might reasonably be called ownership, except as much land as necessity requires for the integrity and proper seclusion of the monastery, and this land may not be cultivated except as a garden for the needs of the sisters. (*CA:ED*, pp. 118–19)

Francis had an abhorrence of personal property. If ever he met someone on the road more destitute than himself, he felt compelled to give that person something, even the cloak around his shoulders, regardless of whether the garment actually belonged to him in the first place. He once said that he had to give away his coat because he only had it on loan from the poor person in front of him, and he needed to return it to its rightful owner. For Francis, property not shared was a kind of theft, an appropriation to oneself of something for which others had a greater need (*FA:ED*, vol. 2, p. 304), thus echoing the earlier teaching of Saints Ambrose of Milan and Basil of Caesarea. The warning of Francis to Clare and her sisters, that they should 'never depart from this by reason of the teaching or advice of anyone' was an oblique reference to Pope Gregory IX, formerly Cardinal Hugolino. Despite his deep respect and affection for Clare and her sisters, Gregory was reluctant to allow any community of religious sisters to live without adequate endowments that would enable them to be self-supporting. The pope didn't want to be responsible for destitute nuns, and it wasn't until 1253, as she lay dying, that Clare was finally able to receive a signed papal instruction allowing her to maintain the 'Privilege of Poverty'. This precious document was the guarantee that Clare and her sisters would always be dependent on the generosity of others and so imitate the poverty of Jesus Christ and his mother. It was enshrined in Clare's *Form of Life*, the Rule that Clare wrote for her sisters. This *Form of Life* drew from the rules already written for them by several popes, but maintained enough of Clare's distinctive spirituality to qualify as the first rule written for women by a woman. Ironically, it was short-lived. Clutched in the hands of the dying Clare in 1253 and signed by Pope Innocent IV, nonetheless, within ten years it had been replaced by another rule issued by the Church, as the inexorable tendency to unify and order the religious life in the Church continued. It is even debateable whether Clare's

'Privilege of Poverty' was ever 'filed' in the appropriate Vatican department or was just given as a gesture to support her in the light of her imminent death and almost certain canonization.

Clare's attitude, as recorded in her *Form of Life*, was that she and her sisters should consider themselves as pilgrims and strangers in this world, travelling light and keeping their eyes on the heavenly kingdom awaiting them where their true riches were to be found. She called her sisters 'heiresses and queens of the kingdom of heaven' (*CA:ED*, pp. 119–20). They should confidently send for alms, that is, have sisters from their community, or Franciscan brothers acting on their behalf, who would go out into the town to beg for whatever the householders could spare. At the same time, the sisters would make church vestments to be distributed wherever there was need, and grow vegetables in the small plot of land they allowed themselves to maintain.

Enclosed in the love of God

Talk of sisters going out to ask for alms begs another question: were not nuns in monasteries strictly forbidden to leave the monastic enclosure? Was this not a fundamental difference between the charisms of Francis and Clare: that the brothers followed Francis in taking the whole world for their cloister, while the sisters with Clare remained securely in one place all their lives? Certainly, the *Form of Life of St Clare* has a formidable passage on keeping the front door shut:

> Let the door be well secured by two different iron locks, with bars and bolts, so that, especially at night, it may be locked with two keys, one of which the portress may have, the other the abbess. During the day let it never be left without a guard and securely locked with one key.
>
> Let them most diligently take care to see that the door is never left open, except when this cannot be conveniently avoided. Let it never be opened to anyone who wishes to

enter, except to those who have been given permission by the Supreme Pontiff or our Lord Cardinal. The sisters may not allow anyone to enter the monastery before sunrise or to remain within after sunset, unless demanded by a manifest, reasonable, and unavoidable cause. (*CA:ED*, p. 124)

But then this was a violent age, and even within the gates of Assisi, as in so many Italian towns of the time, those who could afford it would build defensive towers next to their houses. More than once, troops loyal to Emperor Frederick II attacked Assisi to reclaim it from the authority of the papacy. On one of these occasions the soldiers leaped over the walls of Clare's monastery of San Damiano and were only turned back by the forbidding frown on the forehead of the Lady Clare, brandishing nothing more than a pyx containing the Blessed Sacrament of the Eucharist.

In other parts of the *Form of Life*, it is clear that there is some coming and going into the town by the sisters of the monastery:

The sisters who serve outside the monastery may not delay for long unless some manifest necessity requires it. Let them conduct themselves virtuously and say little, so that those who see them may always be edified. Let them strictly beware of having suspicious meetings or dealings with others. They may not be godmothers of men or women lest gossip or trouble arise because of this. Let them not presume to repeat the gossip of the world inside the monastery. Let them be strictly bound not to repeat outside the monastery anything that is said or done within which could cause scandal. (*CA:ED*, p. 122)

Clearly the sisters were able to visit the town and have conversations long enough to verge into gossip if they were not careful; if there were no danger of this there would have been no need for a warning not to stray too far. It may be that particular individuals were chosen for this responsible work, known as 'extern sisters', but Clare doesn't specify this or say how long a sister should retain such a post. In the witness statements at the Process for Canonization of Clare, one of the sisters remembers that Clare even encouraged the sisters to enjoy their trips out:

> She also said when the most holy mother used to send the serving sisters outside the monastery, she reminded them to praise God when they saw beautiful trees, flowers, and bushes; and, likewise, always to praise him for and in all things when they saw all peoples and creatures. (CA:ED, p. 189)

Perhaps this was an echo of the 'Canticle of the Creatures', composed by Francis in the garden of the San Damiano monastery, exhorting all things to praise God. At the very least it shows that Clare's life was by no means an escape from the world into isolation. She may have opted out of the obligations of feudal family ties, but she had chosen instead a new way of being family, and in fact many of her blood relatives joined her in this alternative way of living together. Throughout their life in community there was hardly a moment of privacy, with common dormitories, chanting the Daily Office of prayers together and working side by side in the garden. And this sense of community extended into relations with the rest of the town of Assisi, particularly when the sisters dedicated themselves to pray for the safety of the townspeople when threatened by invading armies.

Living and working for the benefit of others and sharing the gospel of Christ may even have been expressed in a very radical way in the early days of the community gathered together with Clare. There is a letter written by Bishop Jacques de Vitry, dated 1216, four years after Clare had left her family home, which seems to envisage a quite different way of living in community. He calls them 'Lesser Brothers' and 'Lesser Sisters', and says that they were held in great esteem by the pope and the cardinals:

They live according to the form of the primitive Church, about whom it was written: The community of believers were of one heart and one mind. During the day they go into the cities and villages giving themselves over to the active life in order to gain others; at night, however, they return to their hermitage or solitary places to devote themselves to contemplation. The women dwell together near the cities in various hospices, accepting nothing, but living by the work of their hands. They are grieved, indeed troubled, by the fact that they are honoured by both clergy and laity more than they would wish. (*FA:ED*, vol. 1, pp. 579–80)

At first sight this seems a very egalitarian mode of living in community – men and women together as brothers and sisters. Was this the original vision of Francis and Clare, and an essential aspect of what it meant to be a Franciscan? Did both sisters and brothers work outside their convents, sharing in the ministry of preaching and manual work? But, as pointed out by Franciscan scholar Catherine Mooney (2016, pp. 46–8), the text is not quite so clear. For one thing, although in many documents Francis calls his brothers 'Lesser Brothers' (friars minor), Clare in her Rule and letters never calls her companions 'Lesser Sisters'. In fact, there is no mention of the name of either Francis or Clare in this passage – perhaps it relates to another group, or to the movement overall, of which there were many small and separate gatherings of people dedicated to poverty, prayer and sharing the word of God. Also, there are several places where the word 'they' could refer to either brothers or sisters. Perhaps the brothers went out to work and preach, while the sisters stayed in the hospices and cared for the sick.

But what this passage does show is that it was indeed possible for women and men to work together, to share the same inspiration and to support each other in their ministries. There was cultural space for Francis and Clare to share a common commitment to poverty, prayer and the gospel, even if lived out in different ways. The reservations about contact between men and women, as seen in the Franciscan *Rule of 1223*, were not necessarily the only point of view. In the *Rule* we read Francis encouraging what seems a very defensive view of possible relations between the sexes:

> I strictly command all the brothers not to have any suspicious dealings or conversations with women, and they may not enter the monasteries of nuns, excepting those brothers to whom special permission has been granted by the Apostolic See; and they may not be godfathers to men or women, so that scandal may not arise among the brothers or concerning them on account of this. (*FA:ED*, vol. 1, p. 106)

However, towards the end of Francis' life, we find a much more positive, supportive attitude towards Clare and her sisters in 'The Canticle of Exhortation for the Ladies of San Damiano' (1225):

> Listen, little poor ones called by the Lord,
> who have come together from many parts and provinces.
> Live always in truth,
> that you may die in obedience.
> Do not look at the life without,
> for that of the Spirit is better.
> I beg you out of great love,
> to use with discernment
> the alms the Lord gives you.
> Those weighed down by sickness
> and the others wearied because of them,
> all of you: bear it in peace.
> For you will sell this fatigue at a very high price
> and each one will be crowned queen
> in heaven with the Virgin Mary.
> (*FA:ED*, vol. 1, p. 115)

Here Francis exhorts his sisters 'out of great love' to fulfil their promises in the Lord. They are to look within their hearts (rather than just within the cloister) for that which is of the

Spirit. Francis acknowledges the sickness he is currently suffering from, and is aware of their concern, being looked after in
a temporary shelter made by Clare in the garden of the monastery at San Damiano at the very time this blessing was written.
But his counsel is to bear all things in peace and see such trials
as only increasing the riches stored up in heaven. There was in
any case not much alternative, given the state of medical care
available at the time, but the point was rather to allow all such
suffering to unite one with the suffering Christ. All things in
this life lead to the cross for Francis and Clare as they follow
in the footsteps of Jesus; but the cross itself is also the way to
eternal fellowship with God. It is in the care we show each
other when in pain that the true Kingdom of Heaven is to be
found; and as Clare's sisters later testified, Clare was always
attentive to the needs of her sisters – washing their feet and
their clothing, encouraging them not to fast to excess, a counsel she herself only followed on the strict orders of Francis and
the pope.

This care for each other, which Francis compared to the
compassion a mother would have for her only son, marks a
distinctive element in the lives of both Francis and Clare, and
was just one of the ways in which they supported each other.
In *The Form of Life*, Clare speaks of the mutual support of
brothers and sisters in the Franciscan Orders:

> We ask as a favour of the same Order a chaplain and a clerical
> companion of good reputation, of prudent discernment, and
> two lay brothers, lovers of a holy and upright way of life, in
> support of our poverty, as we have always mercifully had
> from that Order of Lesser Brothers, in the light of the piety of
> God and our blessed Francis. (*CA:ED*, p. 125)

That means there would always be four Franciscan brothers at
any community linked to the Second Order sisters as founded
by Clare at San Damiano. Such a presence came in handy on
more than one occasion. One of the sisters later remembered
that once, on opening the front door, the whole door fell onto

Clare, pinning her down by its weight. It took two burly friars to lift the door off her, luckily being at hand to do so. Maybe the front door was not so secure after all. On another occasion, it was Clare rather than the brothers who went out to repel the Saracen mercenaries as they leaped over the wall of the monastery during the incursions of the Emperor Frederick. Maybe the brothers were out collecting alms at the time, or hiding in the chapel!

Dreaming of Francis

The strength of the connection with Francis, felt by Clare, can be gauged by an extraordinary dream that was recounted to Sister Filippa, the third witness recorded in *The Acts of the Process of Canonization of Clare of Assisi*:

> Lady Clare also related how once, in a vision, it seemed to her she brought a bowl of hot water to Saint Francis along with a towel for drying his hands. She was climbing a very high stairway, but was going very quickly, almost as though she were going on level ground. When she reached Saint Francis, the saint bared his breast and said to the Lady Clare: 'Come, take, and drink.' After she had sucked from it, the saint admonished her to imbibe once again. After she did so what she had tasted was so sweet and delightful she in no way could describe it. After she had imbibed, that nipple or opening of the breast from which the milk comes remained between the lips of blessed Clare. After she took what remained in her mouth in her hands, it seemed to her it was gold so clear and bright that everything was seen in it as in a mirror. (*CA:ED*, p. 161)

Of course, such a dream could well be interpreted in a Freudian way, emphasizing the erotic connection between the two saints. But the sisters with whom Clare shared this vision would have had their own understanding of its significance, based on the religious allusions throughout the vision. It begins with Clare bringing a bowl of water to Francis to wash his hands, perhaps alluding to the washing of the feet of Jesus at Bethany, or the washing of the disciples' feet by Jesus, both recorded in the Gospel of John. Clare is seen as physically intimate with Francis, sharing in his ritual purification. Then in the dream, Clare ascends a stairway, perhaps as if moving beyond the more physical levels of experience, up to the spiritual realms, accompanied by angels 'ascending and descending upon the Son of Man' (John 1.51).

Clare suckling from the breast of Francis would imply her status as an intimate disciple of Francis, nourished and sustained by him. In medieval times, babies were entirely dependent for survival on a mother's milk. It was life-giving, life itself. Christ is therefore offering new life to Clare, through the agency of Francis. Biblical parallels can be found in the prophet Isaiah 66.10–11, the people being nursed and satisfied by the 'consoling breast' of Jerusalem; or in the saying of Paul that he had fed the Corinthians with milk, not solid food (1 Cor. 3.1–2). Religious images of breastfeeding were not unknown in medieval art, such as the 'Lactation of St Bernard', where the Cistercian abbot Bernard of Clairvaux (1090–1153) is shown being fed by a spurt of milk from the breast of the Blessed Virgin Mary.

Pictorial echoes of this can also be seen in depictions of the crucifixion, where Jesus is shown baring the wound in his side, from which flow blood and water that spiritually nourish the disciples standing at the foot of the cross. The Franciscan Tertiary, Margaret of Cortona, spoke of an instruction from her guardian angel to the same effect, that she should feed at the wounded side of Jesus (see Bevegnati, 2012, p. 71). Both Bonaventure and Angela of Foligno speak of the life-giving wound in the side of Jesus, as we shall see in later chapters.

The portrayal of Jesus as mother was a key element of the work of writers such as Anselm of Canterbury (1033–1109) and Julian of Norwich (1343–1416). The scholar Caroline Walker Bynum writes about this theme in her book *Jesus as*

Mother. The Cistercians in particular often referred to the abbot of a monastery both as the representative of Christ and as a mother to his monks; Francis also, at his first meeting with the pope, referred to himself as a mother hen gathering her chicks under her wings, referencing the saying of Jesus in Luke 13.34: 'Jerusalem, Jerusalem, the city that kills the prophets and stones those who are sent to it! How often have I desired to gather your children together as a hen gathers her brood under her wings, and you were not willing!'

Finally, in Clare's dream, the nipple from which the milk comes remains with Clare and is transformed into a golden mirror. The use of a mirror is another motif frequently employed by Clare, signifying that, in Francis, Clare sees the image of Christ; and, through Francis, Clare finds Christ in all things.

Clare uses the image of a mirror in her *Third Letter to Agnes of Prague*:

Place your mind before the mirror of eternity!
Place your soul in the brilliance of glory!
Place your heart in the figure of the divine substance
and, through contemplation,
transform your entire being into the image
of the Godhead Itself,
so that you too may feel what friends feel
in tasting the hidden sweetness
that, from the beginning,
God himself has reserved for his lovers.
(*CA:ED*, p. 51)

The practice of contemplation is spoken of much more by Clare than by Francis. She uses the image of a mirror to suggest the way in which contemplation invites one to enter a new world. One can go beyond the surface of the glass or, as in those days, the dimly seen reflection in polished metal. The mirror becomes a kind of portal, a means of transformation into what is seen beyond the surface of things. In a later chapter we will see how Bonaventure describes this in his *Journey of the Soul into God* as the discovery of the being and goodness of God both through and in the vast complexity of the created world.

For Clare, this is about being transformed into the image of God, being reconfigured as Christ through the loving gaze of contemplation, seeing in her reflection not herself but Christ, as she writes to Agnes of Prague:

> Happy, indeed, is she to whom it is given to drink at this sacred banquet
> so that she might cling with her whole heart to him
> whose beauty all the blessed hosts of heaven unceasingly admire,
>
> whose tenderness touches,
> whose contemplation refreshes,
> whose kindness overflows,
> whose delight overwhelms,
> whose remembrance delightfully dawns,
> whose fragrance brings the dead to life again,
> whose glorious vision will bring happiness
> to all the citizens of the heavenly Jerusalem,
> which [vision], since he is the radiance of eternal glory
> is the brightness of eternal light and the mirror
> without blemish.
> (*CA:ED*, pp. 54–5)

This kind of sensuous love-lyric is relatively common among the mystics of the medieval age. Christ is seen as the heavenly bridegroom and the human soul as his beloved bride; it is sometimes known as bridal mysticism. It is a literary form not limited to female writers. The Cistercian abbots wrote many series of sermons on the biblical allegory The Song of Solomon, Bernard of Clairvaux famously writing several meditations on the first verse alone: 'Let him kiss me with the kisses of his mouth.'

This style of writing is not very evident in the writings of Francis, though he clearly felt a similar passion towards Christ. Perhaps Francis was so captured by the image of the suffering Christ that he had little emotional energy left for the pleasures of the marriage feast with the heavenly bridegroom. Not till the Lauds of the Franciscan friar Jacopone da Todi, a generation later, do we find a male counterpart to the submersion in love shown by Clare in her letters to Agnes of Prague.

Clare evidently shared her vision of Francis with a number of her sisters, with more than one of the witnesses at the Process of Canonization recounting the details. Why share such an intimate story with a crowded law court, with a bishop seated as judge? Probably because it reaffirms the importance to Clare of being seen as a close disciple of Francis. As her brother and father in the faith, already declared a saint of the Church many years earlier, Francis is being described as Clare's guide and patron, one who guarantees for the Church the sanctity of his follower Clare.

Embracing death together

In late 1226, as the health of Francis began to fail, Clare herself became gravely ill. It was as if their two bodies reacted in sympathy with each other. Fearing that she might even die before Francis, she wrote to him, imploring that they might meet again before the end of their lives. Taking into consideration the severity of both their illnesses, despite their love for each other, Francis felt that a meeting would not be possible. Nonetheless, he wrote to her one last time, as recorded in the *Assisi Compilation*:

> To console her, [Francis] wrote his blessing in a letter and also absolved her from any failings, if she had any, regarding his commands and wishes or the commands and wishes of the Son of God. Moreover, so that she would put aside all her grief and be consoled in the Lord, he, or rather the Spirit of God speaking through him, spoke to the brother she had sent. 'Go and take this letter to Lady Clare, and tell her to put aside all her grief and sorrow over not being able to see me now. Let her be assured that before her death, both she and

her sisters will see me and will receive the greatest consolation from me.' (*FA:ED*, vol. 2, pp. 128–9)

Not long after this, Francis died in the evening of 3 October 1226. His body was carried up to Assisi via the monastery at San Damiano, where Clare and her sisters wept for the loss of their great friend and founder. From this point onwards, Clare's health took a turn for the worse. Already frail and weak from too much fasting, Clare spent the next 27 years, the rest of her life, in a perpetual state of sickness. At this time, her mother joined the community, which already included a number of friends and family of the Lady Clare. Was this to share the duties of looking after her ailing daughter? But although Clare remained physically frail, spiritually she was indomitable, and became a repository of the stories about Francis told and retold by his earliest companions. These friars, including Brothers Leo, Rufino and Angelo, became leaders of the 'spirituals', those friars dedicated to maintaining the Rule of Francis in the spirit of the *Testament*, as described in Chapter 1 of this book.

It was this circle of friends that cherished many of the stories recorded in the fourteenth-century text known as *The Little Flowers of Saint Francis*. One of them describes a chaste intimacy between Francis and Clare and is a fitting ending to this brief study of Clare and her relationship with Francis and his companions. In this story, Francis is staying in Assisi where he visited Clare frequently to talk about spiritual things. His companions suggest that he share a meal with her, as she had requested many times. After some initial hesitation Francis agrees and suggests a picnic for the two of them, together with their companions:

[Francis said] 'So that she may be even more consoled, I want this meal to be held at Saint Mary of the Angels, since she has been enclosed for a long time in San Damiano, and it will do her good to see the place of Saint Mary, where she was tonsured and became the spouse of Jesus Christ; and there we will eat together in the name of God.'

When the appointed day arrived, Saint Clare with a companion came out from the monastery, was accompanied by companions of Saint Francis, and came to Saint Mary of the Angels. After she devoutly greeted the Virgin Mary in front of her altar, where she had been tonsured and veiled, they took her around to see the place until it was time to eat. And in the meantime Saint Francis had the table prepared on the bare ground, as he usually did. When it was time to eat they sat down together: Saint Clare with Saint Francis; one of the companions of Saint Francis with the companion of Saint Clare; then all the other companions gathered humbly at the table. And as a first course Saint Francis began to speak of God so sweetly, so deeply, and so wonderfully that the abundance of divine grace descended upon them, and all were rapt into God. And while they were enraptured this way, their eyes and hands lifted up to heaven, the people of Assisi and Bettona and those of the surrounding area saw Saint Mary of the Angels burning brightly, along with the whole place and the forest, which was next to the place. It seemed that a great fire was consuming the church, the place and the forest together. For this reason the Assisians in a great hurry ran down there to put out the fire, believing that everything really was burning. But on arriving at the place, not finding anything burning, they went inside and found Saint Francis with Saint Clare and all their companions sitting around that humble table, rapt into God through contemplation. From this they clearly understood that that was divine, not material fire, which God had made appear miraculously, to demonstrate and signify the fire of divine love, burning in the souls of these holy brothers and holy nuns. Then they departed with great consolation in their hearts and with holy edification.

Then, after a long time, Saint Francis and Saint Clare together with the others returned to themselves; and feeling themselves well comforted by spiritual food, they had little concern for bodily food. And thus finishing that blessed meal, Saint Clare, well accompanied, returned to San Damiano. (*FA:ED*, vol. 3, pp. 590–1)

3

The Hermit: Giles of Assisi
(1190–1262)

In Bonaventure's *Major Life of St Francis*, we find an intriguing story recorded for the first time by any of the early biographers of Francis. Perhaps Bonaventure heard it from Clare herself when he went to visit her and the early companions of Francis at the beginning of his time as Minister General of the Order of Friars Minor. It tells of yet another occasion when Francis is trying to discern his true vocation. After many days of prayer, he realizes that he cannot solve this on his own:

> What do you think, brothers, what do you judge better? That I should spend my time in prayer, or that I should travel about preaching? I am a poor little man, simple and unskilled in speech; I have received a greater grace of prayer than of speaking. Also in prayer there seems to be a profit and an accumulation of graces, but in preaching a distribution of gifts already received from heaven. (*FA:ED*, vol. 2, p. 622)

Unable to come to a resolution, Francis entrusted two of his brothers with the task of going to some wise friends to ask for their advice. The people he asked were Brother Sylvester, a hermit living a life of continuous prayer on Mount Subasio above Assisi, and Sister Clare and her companions at the monastery of San Damiano. This wasn't exactly a neutral panel of advisors. Both Sylvester and Clare were dedicated to the practice of contemplative prayer, in just the same way that Francis wished to be. Nonetheless, both came back with the same message: it was God's will that Francis should preach.

When the two brothers returned from their mission to consult with Sylvester and Clare, Francis heard the advice he had been given, and without asking for any further confirmation, leaped to his feet and was back on the road to wherever the Spirit might lead him next.

Francis, in obedience to the wisdom of his friends, chose to preach rather than pray; or rather, he chose to live the fruits of his prayer in the public gaze, with all the distractions and opportunities of a life on the road. But that wasn't the only way it could have gone. In fact, towards the end of his life, Francis spent more and more time in retreat in solitary prayer, fasting and praying in remote hermitages in the hills of Umbria. A number of his earliest companions chose the same path in life. One such was Brother Giles of Assisi.

Giles, Mary and Martha

Giles was one of the first companions of Francis, revered as one of the founders of the Order, together with Leo, Masseo, Rufino and the other close followers of Francis. Brother Ubertino da Casale, one of the leaders of the reformist friars known as the 'Spirituals', said of Giles:

> But who is able to give an adequate account of the saintliness of that holy man Giles? He was the fourth Lesser Brother, the third of the father's true sons. He started out by throwing himself vigorously into the active life. He was a real Martha. He was to be seen as one whose hands were full continually, with so many virtues to be practised, active ministries to be engaged in, like manual labour, looking after lepers, and other humble tasks. He stayed at this until the day he was caught up in contemplation under the influence of Jesus' love, when he appeared to be more at home in the heavenly city than in the earthly one, though still living in the flesh. Many who witnessed it told me, that as soon as the glory of Paradise was mentioned, he went into ecstasy at the pleasure of it ...

It is not possible to give a brief description of the virtues, contemplative life, and almost continuous ecstasy, which this holy father Giles persevered in and practised to the end of his life; the life of holiness he led would require a special volume to itself, and that a big one. (*FA:ED*, vol. 3, pp. 184–5)

As Ubertino says, Giles was the third to join Francis in his great adventure. Before him were Bernard of Quintavalle, once a rich man of Assisi, and Peter di Catanio, a priest and canon lawyer. In contrast, Giles was a simple, uneducated working man. Just a few days after his arrival at the church of St Mary of the Angels, where Francis and his companions were staying, Giles had his first experience of Franciscan life. He and Francis met a poor woman on their way up to Assisi and Francis said to Giles, still in his secular clothes: 'Why don't you give this poor woman your cloak?' Giles promptly and gladly gave away his cloak and in the process was flooded with a great sense of joy. This was his first taste of Franciscan poverty and the savour of it never left his soul (Brooke, 1970, p. 323).

Giles was a very practical man, 'a real Martha' as Ubertino says, referring to the story of Martha and Mary in the Gospel of Luke 10.38–42, where Martha serves Jesus while Mary, the archetypal contemplative, sits at his feet. But the active phase of Giles' life faded away when he was caught up to paradise in his prayers and went into a state of 'almost continuous ecstasy'. That word 'ecstasy' needs to be understood carefully. Today it has connotations of extreme physical pleasure, but for the medieval mystics it was used in a way closer to its literal meaning of 'standing outside' the body (from the Greek: *ekstasis*). Many things could set it off; for Giles just the word 'paradise' was enough, much to the amusement of the local youths who would call out that word just to see Giles' reaction. Thomas of Celano said that receiving, or just seeing, the eucharistic elements at the time of their consecration during the Mass was the trigger for Francis: 'He received Communion frequently and so devoutly that he made others devout, for at the sweet taste of the spotless Lamb he was often rapt in ecstasy as if drunk in the Spirit' (*FA:ED*, vol. 2, p. 598). The original Latin indicates that it was a kind of supra-mental bliss, a 'departure of the mind' (*excessus mentis*) as much as a physical delight. 'Rapture' (*raptus*) implied a use of force by God, to steal away or ravish the soul. In the Latin version of the New Testament, Peter is described as entering a kind of trance (*mentis excessus*) before seeing a vision (Acts 10.10); and Paul describes 'a certain man' (no doubt himself) who was 'caught up (*raptum*) to the third heaven' (2 Cor. 12.2).

To talk of such rarefied experiences of contemplation may seem to set the standard of prayer too high for many people, but they are recorded in the lives of the saints in order to encourage the reader, rather than to dismay. For saintly people at the time of Francis and Giles, entering a kind of rapture in prayer was not unusual; it was to be expected, rather than to be surprised at, and all part of the ascent to heaven. Attempting to climb too high may not be helpful, as modern Health and Safety regulations always tell us, but the delicious fruits of prayer also grow on the lower branches of the tree of life. In prayer it is enough to enter a simple state of rest in the stillness of God, for example through a repeated phrase or word. The rest is all grace, all the gift of an infinitely generous God.

Francis himself practised this form of contemplative prayer. At the beginning of his conversion, it was his use of a mantra or prayer-word throughout the night that convinced Bernard of Quintavalle to give away all his possessions and become Francis' first brother in religion. The phrase Francis used at that time was: '*Deus meus et omnia*', translated as 'My God and All', or 'My God and my All', according to *The Deeds of Blessed Francis and His Companions* (*FA:ED*, vol. 3, p. 437). In a slightly later version of the story, Francis is said to have simply prayed repeatedly, 'My God, my God', according to the Italian text known as *The Little Flowers of Saint Francis* (*FA:ED*, vol. 3, p. 568). On another occasion, Francis used the phrase, 'Lord, be merciful to me a sinner' many times, until a spirit of peace overcame him (*FA:ED*, vol. 1, p. 205). At the La Verna hermitage, Francis repeated the question, over and over: 'Who are you, my dearest God? And what am I?' (Habig, 1973, p. 1444). During this latter retreat he was said to have been seen levitating three or four feet into the air, even getting lost in the branches of a tree. All of which sounds once more beyond the capacities of us lesser mortals, but as the word 'rapture' implies, prayer is God's work, not ours; or as Paul puts it: '... the Spirit helps us in our weakness; for we do not know how to pray as we ought, but that very Spirit intercedes with sighs too deep for words' (Rom. 8.26). According to the biblical scholar Paula Gooder (2006), Paul's description of his experience in prayer as recorded in 2 Corinthians 12.2 may itself be an admission of failure, as if to say: 'Look at me, poor Christian that I am: I only made it to the third heaven; I still have four more heavens to go!'

Action and contemplation

But before these rarefied states of contemplative prayer became frequent, Giles devoted himself to the active life of service and manual work. Indeed, he felt that this was the natural order of the spiritual path and that contemplation depended on action. Giles is recorded as saying:

> Since no one would be able to successfully undertake the contemplative life without first having undergone faithful and dedicated training in the active life, one ought to work hard and diligently in the practice of the active life.
>
> A good practitioner of the active life would be someone who, if it were possible, would feed all the poor people of this world, clothe them all, give them an abundance of everything they need, and build all the churches and hostels and bridges of this world. Then, after all this, if everyone in the world considered them to be bad, and they were well aware of it, they would not want to be considered anything but bad, and would not stop doing any good work on account of this, but would apply themselves with greater fervour to every good work. (Lachance and Brunette, 2015, p. 23)

Active ministry should be done for its own sake, not with the hope of reward. Martha is therefore to be commended because, even though she was rebuked by Jesus for being so busy, still she did not give up her generous ministry of active service. The joy of performing a good deed was in itself a more than sufficient reward. Perhaps it was the experience of living with Giles that made Francis include in his *Earlier Rule*: 'Let the brothers who know how to work do so and exercise that trade they have learned, provided it is not contrary to the good of their souls and can be performed honestly' (*FA:ED*, vol. 1, p. 68). In a rare exception to strict poverty, the *Earlier Rule* goes on to allow the brothers to have the tools necessary for their trades. In his *Testament*, Francis confirms this as his own experience, saying: 'I worked with my hands, and I still desire to work; and I earnestly desire all brothers to give themselves to honest work' (*FA:ED*, vol. 1, p. 125). In this, Francis was following the example of the desert fathers and mothers who often worked with their hands, weaving baskets out of reeds; St Paul also worked as a tentmaker.

Giles was a jack of all trades. When in Ancona en route to the Holy Land, he kept himself busy selling water for bread. At another time he helped bring in the olive harvest, again asking for bread as his wages: like Francis, he did not want to be caught up in the monetary economy. Once, on receiving his wages, he knocked on the door of a cardinal in order to share this meal. Rather nonplussed by the cheek of the offer, the cardinal suggested Giles should receive the bread that he, the cardinal, gave to the poor. In reply Giles quoted Psalm 128 about happily eating the fruit of one's own labours, and, tearing off a chunk of his loaf, left the cardinal to fix his own lunch.

Pilgrimage was a favourite occupation of Giles, who journeyed to St James Compostela in Spain and to various shrines in southern Italy. When Giles returned to Assisi, Francis could see that Giles was a man who knew his own mind and set his own course, so he left him free to decide where he wanted to go next. Giles answered that he didn't want such complete freedom but would rather go wherever Francis might send him. Perhaps discerning within Giles a latent gift of prayer, Francis sent him to a hermitage at Fabione near the Umbrian city of Perugia. It was a posting that turned his life around.

Ecstasy and rapture

In the *Life of Blessed Brother Giles*, probably written by Brother Leo, a friend of Giles and the close companion of Francis, we see a moment of conversion:

> Among other favours which the Lord bestowed on [Giles], was that one night when he was at prayer, he was filled with divine grace and consolation so utterly that it seemed to him that the Lord wished to draw his soul out of his body so that he might see his secrets clearly and that he might be inspired to labour better and grow stronger in the service of God. He began to experience from his feet up how it feels when the body dies after the spirit has left it. His soul stood outside his body, as it pleased our Creator, who had put it in the body, and was charmed to behold itself, so very beautifully was it adorned by the Holy Spirit. It was slender and bright beyond valuation as he himself admitted near his death. That most holy spirit was rapt in contemplation of heavenly secrets, which he revealed to no one. 'Blessed is the man who knows how to guard and keep safe the secrets of God, since nothing is hidden which will not be revealed as and when God pleases. But I fear for myself,' he said, 'and if they are revealed I should prefer them to be revealed through another, not through me.' (Brooke, 1970, p. 327)

Here again we have reference to an experience of ecstasy or rapture. It seems to be a classic 'out of body' experience, or even a near-death experience, perhaps triggered by a regime of fasting, sleep deprivation through night vigils in prayer and long periods of silence and solitude at the hermitage where he was now staying. Francis had himself written a short rule for those brothers who wished to live in hermitages, where these types of experiences might be more likely to occur. Francis said that they should be small communities of three or at most four brothers, the better to keep to a simple, poor style of living. The brothers should be divided into 'mothers' and 'sons', the former doing the cooking and cleaning and answering the door, with the latter free to devote themselves to contemplation. Periodically the friars should exchange roles, so that all would be given the chance to go as far as they could in the practice of prayer. A strict enclosure should be observed, with no one allowed in to eat with the brothers and no hint of gossip or worldly talk allowed. It was the kind of life Francis himself would have liked to follow, and which he did join during the several 40-day retreats he allowed himself each year. This would have been the style of life at the hermitage of La Verna, where Francis received the stigmata, the wounds of Christ in his own body. It was also the sort of life he advocated for the community at St Mary of the Angels, the centre of the Order he founded and the model Franciscan friary.

Leo said that Giles was 'rapt in contemplation of heavenly secrets, which he revealed to no one'. In part this was a reference back to Paul's vision recounted in 2 Corinthians, where he 'heard things that are not to be told, that no mortal is permitted to repeat' (v. 4). But it may also be a reference to Francis, who was himself very reticent to speak about the stigmata, the signs of crucifixion formed in his own body after a long retreat at the hermitage of La Verna. As Thomas of Celano explains: 'In every way possible [Francis] tried to hide these marks, so that human favour would not rob him of the grace given him. He would never or rarely reveal his secret to anyone' (*FA:ED*, vol. 1, p. 265). In this passage, Celano goes on to describe how Francis explained his reluctance to speak of these mysteries with a quote from the Scriptures: 'He always carried in his heart and often had on his lips the saying of the prophet: "I have hidden your words in my heart to avoid any sin against you"' (Ps. 119.11). This reticence about speaking of

revelations received in prayer is a repeated theme in the sayings
of Brother Giles:

> After this the holy brother Giles concentrated all his efforts on
> preserving carefully the grace which God had given him. He
> used to say that understanding how to guard the grace given to
> him by God was more important than any other grace or virtue.
> 'This is what matters most.' Then he said: 'After the Apostles
> received the gift of the Holy Spirit they carried a weight – a
> hundred, a thousand times greater in bearing tribulations and
> preserving the grace given them.' From then on he was always
> and always has been in his cell alone, keeping watch, fasting,
> praying, scrupulously guarding himself from all evil deeds
> and words. If ever anyone wanted to tell blessed brother Giles
> about somebody's evil ways, he would say this to him: 'I do
> not want to know another's sin.' He would say to the gossip:
> 'Take care, brother, that you do not see what is prejudicial,
> and will not profit you.' (Brooke, 1970, pp. 333–5)

Giles was careful to 'guard the grace given to him' by not
speaking openly about his experiences in prayer, but this does
not mean that he was trying to hide away from the world. He
describes the Spirit-filled mission of the apostles as itself an
exercise in preserving the grace given to them. Although the
apostles may not have spoken much about the actual experience of receiving the Holy Spirit at Pentecost, a kind of rapture
enabling them to speak in other languages, still they allowed
that experience to energize them for the world-wide mission of
spreading the gospel of God's kingdom inaugurated in the life,
death and resurrection of Jesus Christ. Giles is referencing the
experience of Pentecost as the archetypal Christian rapture, a
positive energy not spoken of directly but allowed to transform the world around each Spirit-filled believer. For Giles,
this mission inspired by the Holy Spirit entailed giving spiritual
direction to his brothers, including hearing the confession of
sins and the offer of counsel – provided it was their own sins
that his visitors wanted to confess and not the sins of others!

Having said this, Giles was 'not backward in coming forward', as the saying goes, about criticizing his brothers when he thought it was due. After the death of Francis, when Brother Elias was leading the friars, and building a massive basilica in Assisi to house the relics of St Francis, together with a friary for the brothers, Giles let his opinion of this grand building project be known:

When Brother Giles once came to Assisi, the friars took him round their new home, showing him the splendid buildings which they had put up, and apparently taking great pride in them. But when Brother Giles had carefully looked at them all, he said to the brethren: 'You know, brethren, there's only one thing you're short of now, and that's wives!' The brothers were deeply shocked at this; so Brother Giles said to them: 'My brothers, you know well enough that it is just as illegal for you to give up poverty as to give up chastity. After throwing poverty overboard it is easy enough to throw chastity as well.' (Habig, 1972, p. 1843)

Struggling with the devil

Ecstatic raptures of grace-filled bliss were by no means the only adventures in prayer that Giles experienced. Sometimes he had distinctly dark moments of fear, even terror:

One night as blessed brother Giles prayed to God, the devil wanted to hamper the blessing God poured on him. Giles was so gripped with fear that he began to scream: 'Help, brothers, help.' His call woke brother Gratian, who was near him in another cell, and he got up quickly and came to him calling loudly: 'Never fear, never fear, father. I am coming to help you.' Arriving at his cell he said: 'What was the matter, father?' 'Don't worry, my son, don't worry.' Gratian replied: 'Let me stay with you, as the enemy persecutes you so sore.' Giles replied: 'The Lord reward you, my son. You did well to come to me but go now and return to your place.' Yet when in the evening he prepared to return to his cell after the meal he said: 'I expect martyrdom.' (Brooke, 1970, p. 345)

Often these attacks by evil forces were experienced as physical debilitation. Once when praying in a church at Spoleto, he found himself unable to straighten up, just managing to shuffle along to a holy water stoop where he could splash himself with the blessed water and set himself free. Another time he felt as if he were in an enclosed space, unable to get free. Finally, his cries for help were answered by a brother who had to force open the door of his cell with all his strength. In these stories, Giles is seen as following the example of his mentors in the faith, Francis and Clare of Assisi. Francis complained several times of the tricks played on him by the demons and the fear that often accompanied these dark moments.

> [Francis] used to struggle hand to hand with the devil who, in those places, would not only assault him internally with temptations but also frighten him externally with ruin and undermining. The brave soldier of God knew that his Lord could do all things in all places; thus he did not give in to the fears but said in his heart: 'You, evil one! You cannot strike me with your evil weapons here anymore than if we were in front of a crowd in a public place.' (*FA:ED*, vol. 1, p. 244)

In the early days of his conversion, Francis had a particular fear that lodged in his mind. His attention was drawn to a disfigured hunchback woman of Assisi, whose looks scared the people of the town. The devil threatened that Francis too would be disfigured in this way if he didn't abandon his resolve to live the life to which God had called him. But Francis drew the same moral from the experience as he would soon afterwards with the leper that he embraced – he freely chose what was bitter, that the bitter might become sweet (see *FA:ED*, vol. 2, p. 248). Overcoming fear and aversion was a large part of his spiritual path and one that brought him great joy.

Such struggles with the devil are reminiscent of the stories and sayings of the desert fathers and mothers – hermits living in the deserts of Egypt, Palestine and Syria from the third century onwards. Their experiences were typified by Anthony the Great, whose life story, written by Athanasius of Alexandria, became one of the bestsellers of its day. Throughout the Middle Ages these sayings would be told and retold by monastics, their teaching being codified by monks like Evagrius Ponticus and John Cassian. In his early days in the desert, Anthony was plagued by visions of strange and terrifying beasts, as if they were hurling themselves at him out of the walls of the Egyptian tomb in which he was learning the arts of contemplative prayer. But this wasn't the end of the story. After travelling progressively further into the silence of the desert, Anthony eventually emerged radiantly healthy both in mind and body. Having scoured the depths of his own soul he could read in the furrows of their brow the sorrows and pains of those who came to him for counsel. When asked how he could live in such a deserted place with no books, he replied: 'My book is the whole created world: what need do I have of other books?'

Professor at the School of Prayer

So, too, Giles emerged from his years of penitential struggle with sound and gentle advice to those who sought him out:

> On another occasion someone told him, 'What can I do? If I do something good, I get vain about it. And if I do something bad, I get sad and almost despair.' Holy brother Giles answered, 'You do well to feel sorrow for your sin. However, I advise you to feel sad with moderation; you must always believe that God's power to pardon is greater than your power to sin. And if God grants mercy to any great sinner, do you believe he will abandon a small sinner? Also, do not stop doing good because you are tempted by vainglory. If a

farmer, about to sow seed in the ground, said to himself, "I don't want to sow this year because birds may come and eat my grain," and because of that, he didn't sow, he would have no produce from his land to eat. But if he sows, although he might lose a little, still the greater part would be his. That is the way it is with the one who is tempted by vainglory but fights it.' (Lachance and Brunette, 2015, p. 20)

Vainglory was one of the Eight Thoughts (Greek: *Logismoi*) taught by Evagrius, in his prefiguring of the 'seven deadly sins' listed by Gregory the Great two centuries later. It was seen as one of the most difficult sins to overcome, sneaking up on the unsuspecting monastic when in their own eyes they seemed to have finally achieved something in their practice of prayer. But that should not be a reason for despair, itself one of the principal thoughts according to the desert tradition. Just discard all comparisons with others and maintain humility at all times, always returning to a simple prayer for grace, like the ancient prayer that asks the Lord for mercy: *kyrie eleison*!

Giles had a way of finding just the right metaphor in his teaching, evoking something visible that stays in the mind. On another occasion he taught the virtue of patience, no doubt from his own experience:

One of the brothers told him, 'A person should find it very painful when they cannot find in prayer the grace of devotion.' Brother Giles responded, 'I advise you to go slow on this matter. For if you knew there was some good wine in a cask and there was a sediment at the bottom, would you shake the cask and mix the wine with the sediment? That would not be the thing to do. And if the grindstone of a mill sometimes does not make good flour the miller does not immediately smash it with a hammer, but he repairs the grindstone slowly and gradually, and then it makes good flour.' (Lachance and Brunette, 2015, p. 20)

But the gradual, patient labour of sifting the contents of the mind and heart eventually brought great rewards to Brother Giles, not least in the revelations of self-knowledge:

> Many special favours are obtained and many good habits are established in the course of prayer. To start off with: a man's mind is enlightened and his faith is warmed up. He gets to know his own deficiencies. He acquires fear of God and humility. He goes down in his own estimation and gains heartfelt sorrow. Later, he gets a sensitive conscience, he steadies himself patiently, he obeys joyfully. He comes to acquire genuine discretion, knowledge, understanding, and fortitude. He reaches wisdom and that knowledge of God which is revealed to those 'who adore him in spirit and in truth' (John 4.24). Then a man experiences the excitement of love and races toward the aroma of the Beloved. At last he reaches a pleasant sweetness, his mind is plunged in a vast peace, and finally he arrives at the glory of his homeland. (Giles, 1990, p. 105)

Giles was a practitioner of a wisdom rooted in self-awareness. Abstract knowledge was of no use to him, and so he was particularly distrustful of an education that exalted the student or professor rather than guiding one directly to the true knowledge of God. To this end he was sharply critical of theology acting as a distraction leading to pride. He is famously recorded as saying against the Franciscan students at Paris university: 'Paris! Paris! You are demoralizing the Order of St Francis!' Giles was not afraid of questioning the value of academic honours, as Ubertino da Casale said of him:

> Here was a man who, when he saw aspiring lectors or those ambitious to do studies, would, mockingly, make a trumpet of his two fists. This study and science of theirs, he would elucidate, was all for celebrity and worldly flourish, like the hollow sound of a trumpet! (FA:ED, vol. 3, p. 184)

To a friar about to preach Giles gave the advice that he should say: '*Bo, bo, molto dico, poco fo*' (Blah, blah, I talk a lot but scarce do a jot). Or just as pungently: '*Fate, fate, non parlate!*' (Work, work! Don't talk!) (Giles, 1990, p. 120). But when he explains his point a bit further, the truth of his words is undeniable:

> A man who is avid of profound learning ought to work very hard and keep himself close to the earth. Then God will give him plenty of knowledge. The loftiest wisdom consists in accomplishing good deeds, guarding oneself, and pondering God's point of view ... God's word does not become the possession of him who hears it or preaches it, but of him who lives it. (Giles, 1990, pp. 90–1)

For all his bluster, Giles was not a man who disapproved of books as such, just the misuse of academic qualifications in order that they might be a source of pride. In this he was a true son of St Francis, who once wrote to the great Franciscan theologian and preacher Anthony of Padua: 'I am pleased that you teach sacred theology to the brothers providing that, as is contained in the Rule, you "do not extinguish the Spirit of prayer and devotion" during study of this kind' (*FA:ED*, vol. 1, p. 107). Francis always wanted his brothers to be 'lesser brothers', 'friars minor', not exalted by titles and deference. Humility as a virtue always trumped status in society for Francis, and he would have warmed to the teaching of Giles that Scripture should first be lived before it was preached.

Contemplative guide

Nonetheless, acuteness of mind was not to be despised. One particular saying shows that Giles was capable of drawing fine distinctions in the elucidation of the contemplative path:

There are seven levels of contemplation: fire, anointing, ecstasy, contemplation, taste, rest, and glory. I say *fire*: that is, the light that precedes the enlightenment of the soul. Then, *anointing* with ointments, from which there rises a marvellous fragrance, which follows that light; as it says in the Song of Songs (1.3), *In the fragrance of your ointments*, and so on. After this, *ecstasy*, for when the fragrance is experienced, the soul is snatched up and taken away from the senses of the body. Then *contemplation* follows, for after the soul is drawn away from the bodily senses, it contemplates God in a marvellous way. After this comes *taste*, for in contemplation the soul experiences a wondrous sweetness, about which the Psalm (34.8) speaks: *Taste and see*, and so on. Next *rest*, for when the spiritual palate has been sweetened, the soul rests in that sweetness. Finally, *glory* follows, for the soul glories in such rest and is refreshed with tremendous joy; whence the Psalm (16.11) says, *I will have everything I could want, when your glory appears*. (Lachance and Brunette, 2015, pp. 21–2)

This passage is quoted by Bonaventure in his *Commentary on the Gospel of Luke* (chapter IX, 48), and referred to in a more detailed discussion in his 'Sermon 1 on the Holy Sabbath'. It also appears in a short treatise called *On the Seven Steps of Contemplation*, formerly attributed to Bonaventure, but now seen as being authored by the Victorine scholar Thomas Gallus (c. 1200–1246). As such it is an important passage in that it shows the close inter-connections of Franciscan spirituality with that of the Abbey of St Victor in Paris. The Victorines, especially Hugh and Richard of St Victor, were very influential on Franciscan authors such as Bonaventure. They were famous in their day for their intricate systems of allegorical biblical interpretation that mapped out the stages of the spiritual ascent in great detail.

Here in this passage from the sayings of Brother Giles there is a delightful interplay of the role of the physical and spiritual senses in the path to contemplation. First there is *fire*, perhaps like that described by the English fourteenth-century hermit

Richard Rolle, who wrote of the warmth he felt in his chest when at prayer, a transfigured sense of touch or warmth (Latin: *calor*) combined with sweetness (*dulcor*) and song (*canor*). Then there is *anointing* 'with a marvellous fragrance', the sense of smell being purified and sweetened. This leads to *ecstasy*, the rapture we have already encountered in the writings about Giles, where the physical senses are left behind and the spiritual senses come to the fore. Next comes *contemplation*, the sense of sight being opened up to see the invisible God in and through the visible creation. Then comes *taste*, a lingering savour of the sweetness of God's presence. Next there is *rest*, the chance to enjoy the refined sense of sweet contentment in prayer. Finally, there is the stage of *glory*, where the soul is refreshed in peace and a 'tremendous joy'.

Reading through this gradual transformation of the senses brings home the teaching that for the medieval mystics, Franciscans among them, the experience of prayer was one of great delight. Of course, it was based on the discipline and hard work of the recital of the psalms and the reading of the Scriptures in the Daily Office and there was no escape from the patient transformation of the mind in the cleansing of sin; but at the end of the process there is nothing but joy. And this is not a kind of solipsistic self-centred happiness, but a sharing in the glory of the saints and angels and all the company of heaven. As Psalm 16, quoted by Giles, also says: 'As for the holy ones in the land, they are the noble, in whom is all my delight' (Ps. 16.3). Visions experienced by Francis and his followers almost invariably involve a sight of a procession of saints, led by Jesus and his blessed mother, all in the shining robes of glory.

Among writers on contemplative prayer, the description of a sequence of stages is not uncommon. For example, Teresa of Avila (1515–1582) writes of the Interior Castle, with its seven 'mansions' or courts leading into the throne room of God; while John of the Cross (1542–1591) writes of the successive stages of the dark nights of the senses and the soul. Other religious traditions have comparable maps of the spiritual terrain, such as the ten *Sephirot*, emanations and attributes of God in the Kabbalah tradition of Judaism, or the eight states of meditative absorption (Sanskrit: *dhyāna*) described in Buddhism. In these teachings, the initial euphoria becomes progressively calmed and refined until there is an abiding sense of peace and a clarity of mind that knows directly of a joy-filled intuition of the way things are.

Giles himself speaks of this joy, albeit tinged with a certain sorrow that he hadn't abandoned himself fully to that joy of the Holy Spirit earlier in his life:

> Once near his death as he was returning from his cell filled with unspeakable joy, he said to one of his companions; 'My son, what does it seem to you that this may be? For I found a great treasure, so bright and so splendid that I cannot find words to describe it. I am wasting it, my son, I am wasting it. But tell me, as you are inspired by God, how you interpret it.' Many times he repeated this, and as he said it he was so full of joy and fervour that he seemed as if drunk with the Holy Spirit. (Brooke, 1970, pp. 345-7)

In the end, Giles knew the inebriation in the blood of Christ, spoken of by the medieval Christian prayer known by its opening words: '*Anima Christi*'. Giles had drunk a full draft of Christ, and still stood on his feet, or rather knelt before his God. He may not have talked much about Francis, but he was consciously following in the footsteps of the *poverello* of Assisi. Some may say that Francis sought martyrdom early in his life, but after his final retreat at La Verna, he lived a kind of martyrdom every day, bearing the wounds of Jesus in his own body. Giles was not dissimilar:

> When a brother once mentioned to him that St Francis had said that a servant of God ought always to desire to die, and to die a martyr's death, he replied: 'For myself, I do not wish to die a better death than one of contemplation.' At one time indeed he had gone to the Saracens, desiring martyrdom for the love of Christ, but after he returned and was found

69

worthy to ascend to the height of contemplation, he said: 'I should not have wished then for a martyr's death.' (Brooke, 1970, p. 347)

Giles was a martyr to contemplation, making an offering of himself in his own particular way. Perhaps Francis always knew that would be the case when he first sent him off to a hermitage to explore first hand the contemplative life. Being Franciscan, for Giles, meant renouncing the world for a life of silence and solitary prayer. But he was no less Franciscan for that. Maybe Francis envied Giles in a way, himself always having to live up to the sainthood that the crowds thrust upon him. Giles just got on with his life, though his admiration of Francis remained to the end:

> They asked him what he thought of St. Francis, and at the mention of that name he was all aglow. He responded: 'We should not ever mention that man without smacking our lips with relish. He lacked only one thing, a strong body. If he had been robust like me, surely the whole world could never have been able to keep pace with his flaming spirit.' (Giles, 1990, p. 134)

Two meetings and a flowering staff

To end this chapter, I offer two stories about Brother Giles from later collections. One involves a wordless greeting, as befits a hermit committed to silence and solitude; the other a rebuke to a theologian who doubted the perpetual virginity of the Blessed Virgin Mary. Perhaps the reader will say, 'But this can't be true! These are children's stories!' I can only respond, 'They may not be strictly historical, but is there no truth to be found in them?' The Franciscan tradition is a story-telling tradition. Stories live by being retold in each generation, and in the retelling, new meanings are always to be found. First, from *The Little Flowers of Saint Francis*, the story of an encounter in

Perugia between Giles and Saint Louis, the King of France and a patron of the Franciscan Third Order.

> Arriving at the door of the place of the brothers like a poor, unknown pilgrim, with few companions, [the king] asked urgently for Brother Giles, not telling the porter anything about who was asking for him. So the porter went to Brother Giles and said that there was a pilgrim at the door who was asking for him; and God inspired him and revealed to him in spirit that it was the King of France. So with great fervour he immediately came out of the cell and ran to the door, and without any further questions, though they had never seen each other, they both knelt down with great devotion, and embraced each other ...
>
> As the King was leaving, a brother asked one of his companions who that man was, who had been embracing Brother Giles, and he replied that it was Louis, King of France, who had come in order to see Brother Giles. When he told this to the other brothers they were very upset that Brother Giles had not spoken a word to him, and they said to him bitterly: 'O Brother Giles, why were you so rude? Here is a king who came from France to see you and to hear some good word from you, and you didn't say anything to him?' Brother Giles replied: 'O dear brothers, don't be surprised at this: he couldn't say a word to me, nor I to him, because as soon as we embraced, the light of divine wisdom revealed and manifested his heart to me, and mine to him; and so, by divine action, as we looked into each other's hearts: whatever I wanted to say to him, or he to me, we already knew much better than if we had spoken with our mouths, and with greater consolation.' (*FA:ED*, vol. 3, p. 625)

And from *The Deeds of the Blessed Francis and his Companions*:

> At one time during Brother Giles's lifetime there was a great Master of the Order of Preachers who for many years

endured the greatest doubt about the virginity of the Mother of Jesus Christ. For it seemed to him that it was impossible for her to be both mother and virgin. Yet, as truly a man full of faith, he grieved over such a doubt as this, and he wished that some inspired man would free him from it. Hearing that Brother Giles was an illustrious man, he went to him.

The holy Brother Giles, knowing in spirit that he was coming, what his purpose was, and the battle he was enduring, went out to meet him. Before he reached the Friar Preacher, he struck the ground with his staff which he carried in his hand, and said: 'O Friar Preacher, a virgin before the birth.' And immediately a very beautiful lily sprang up where Giles struck the ground with his staff. Striking the ground a second time, he said: 'O Friar Preacher, a virgin during the birth!' And another lily sprang up. Striking the ground a third time, he said: 'O Friar Preacher, a virgin after the birth!' And immediately a third lily sprang up. After this, Giles fled.

That Friar Preacher was entirely freed from the temptation, and from then on he always had a great devotion towards the holy Brother Giles. (*FA:ED*, vol. 3, p. 564)

4

The Penitent: Margaret of Cortona
(1247–1297)

The vocation of Francis began with a voice from the cross – Jesus speaking from the crucifix in the dim light of the church of San Damiano – and it came to fruition as he knelt before another cross, this time the vision of an angel on a cross in blazing light at the summit of Mount La Verna. The first encounter wounded Francis' heart with a longing love for his crucified Lord; the second encounter wounded his body with the stigmata, the wounds of the Saviour in his hands, feet and side. In between these two crucifixions, Francis often meditated on the cross. He had even made a special request of the Lord, as related in *The Considerations on the Sacred Stigmata*, an appendix to *The Little Flowers of Saint Francis*. As he began his retreat on Mount La Verna, Francis had prayed:

> My Lord Jesus Christ, I pray you to grant me two graces before I die: the first is that during my life I may feel in my soul and in my body, as much as possible, that pain which you, dear Jesus, sustained in the hour of your most bitter Passion. The second is that I may feel in my heart, as much as possible, that excessive love with which you, O Son of God, were inflamed in willingly enduring such suffering for us sinners. (Habig, 1972, p. 1448)

Margaret of Cortona, a saint of the Third Order of St Francis, followed closely in the footsteps of Francis in her devotion to the crucified Lord, while living the life of a penitent and

73

prayerful recluse. As a young woman, Margaret was known for her beauty and her pride. She lived for several years as the paramour of a nobleman of Montepulciano by the name of Arsenio, to whom she bore a son. Wealthy and secure, she seemed to have everything, with fine clothes and rich foods, and the company of a man who loved her, though apparently not enough to formalize their relationship in marriage. Perhaps her low-born status was too much of a barrier to their being registered as man and wife. But Margaret's life fell apart with the sudden death of her lover in a robbery or some kind of vendetta; his dog returned alone from a hunting trip and plaintively led Margaret back to Arsenio's broken body. Margaret was about 25 years old when this calamity happened, and having been disowned by her family, she came to Cortona, where she lived the rest of her life. There she threw herself on the mercy of two noblewomen of the town – the countess Marinaria and her daughter-in-law Ranieria. These two offered Margaret a room for her and her son, and found her a job as a midwife.

Soon Margaret was drawn to the Order of Franciscan Penitents, and petitioned the Franciscan friars of the town, asking to be allowed to wear the habit of a penitent of the nascent Third Order. Despite their misgivings, the friars eventually agreed and gave her the use of a room attached to the church of St Francis, where she could attend the services and listen to the friars' sermons. She sent her son, now about 12 years old, to become a novice at the friary in Arezzo. Perhaps the bond between the two was not strong but, whether with his consent or not, Margaret entrusted her son to the friars and from then on he largely fades away from the story of her life.

The origin of the Third Order is recounted in *The Little Flowers of Saint Francis*:

Setting out with an eager spirit, without considering road or path, [Francis, Masseo and Angelo] came to a village called Cannara. And Saint Francis began to preach, and he first commanded the swallows to keep silent until he had finished preaching. And the swallows obeyed him. And he preached there with such fervour that in their devotion all the men and women of that town wanted to follow him and abandon the town. But Saint Francis did not allow them, saying, 'Don't be in a hurry, and don't leave: I'll arrange what you must do for the salvation of your souls.' And then he got the idea of starting the Third Order for the universal salvation of all. And thus he left them much consoled and well disposed towards penance. (*FA:ED*, vol. 3, pp. 592–3)

At first known as The Brothers and Sisters of Penance, they became known as the Third Order in relation to the First Order of brothers, who were also called the Order of Friars Minor, and the Second Order of sisters, known as the Poor Ladies of San Damiano. The Third Order, also known as 'Tertiaries', were men and women, ordained and lay, who were inspired by the example of St Francis to live a life of devotion to God, but without necessarily leaving their homes and families. Some did indeed form or join communities, taking the vows of poverty, chastity and obedience, and these became known as the Third Order Regular, with their own Rule, and so having some autonomy from the established First and Second Orders. Others remained in their existing station of life, whether married or single, being known as Third Order Seculars. Francis gave the Third Order a Rule in 1221 to guide their lives, which was re-affirmed by Pope Nicholas IV in 1289. Later in her life, Margaret was joined by a number of others and together they became a Third Order community, but at the early stage of her vocation she was living more independently.

Now firmly settled in Cortona, Margaret soon became known for her devotional fervour – her prayers and fasting and her dedication to nursing the poor at a hospital she had helped to found. Her wise counsel and care for the sick became the object of both curiosity and admiration. She went to the friars for spiritual guidance, in particular Brother Giunta Bevegnati, who became her spiritual director, confessor and later her biographer. As their relationship developed, Friar Giunta became more and more a partner with Margaret in negotiating the peace of the town with its neighbours, and working for the reconciliation of its people with God:

> Another day Christ said to Margaret: My child, what would you say if the time came that the citizens of Cortona should bless the alms they give you, seeing that you are set as a voice in the wilderness to call them to peace? For I will that you cry 'Peace amongst people' to Cortona; and truly you are sent as a messenger of peace. And this grace I grant to the citizens of Cortona because of the reverent devotion they have shown you. Wherefore tell your confessor to preach publicly in Cortona the message of peace and in my name to invite the people to mutual trust and concord. (Cuthbert, 1900, p. 268)

Just as Francis was called to be a messenger of peace, announcing peace with every sermon and reconciling people to each other, so Margaret and Giunta continued this ministry together. But this situation didn't last for ever. Some of the friars became increasingly uneasy with the relationship between the two and Brother Giunta was limited to seeing Margaret no more than once a week. Margaret herself began to withdraw from her more active ministry, moving to a solitary cell near the city wall, towards the highest point of Cortona. There she gave herself increasingly to a life of prayer and contemplation, with a rich devotional life expressed in conversations she would have with her Lord, which often took place on the feast days of the Church's year.

Finally, Br Giunta was sent away to the Franciscan friary at Siena, only returning to see Margaret as she approached her death seven years later. During this time, Margaret was guided by the rector of St Basilio's Church, Ser Badio. Margaret died on 22 February 1297, which became her unofficial feast day in 1516, though she was not actually canonized until 1728. Some have wondered why she has remained a largely marginal figure in the history of the Franciscans; it may well have been because she was in the shadow of the patrons of the Third

Order, Elizabeth of Hungary (d. 1231) and Louis IX of France (1214–1270). Perhaps it was the misgivings of the friars in her adopted home which told against her recognition as a saint; or the severity of her penitential practices may have allied her too closely to the movement known as the 'spirituals', reformists among the early Franciscans. Occasionally she was even confused with Margaret of Antioch, a saint from a much earlier age. Nevertheless, Margaret soon became the patron of Cortona, and her tomb was built at the church of St Basilio, which was later administered by the Franciscans and dedicated to Santa Margherita. This church became a pilgrimage destination, not least for people seeking healing from diseases of body and mind.

Brother Giunta records a devout conversation between Margaret and her Lord, confirming her in her true status as a light to the Third Order, regardless of the views of those among whom she lived:

> The Lord said: 'Since you have become so humble, you will be exalted among the saints in heaven … You are the third light given to the Order of my blessed Francis. Francis is the first light, in the Order of the Friars Minor. Clare is the second, in the Order of nuns, and you are the third in the Order of penitents.' (Bevegnati, 2012, p. 290)

As a designated penitent, Margaret encouraged others to practise penance and be reconciled to God. She became a kind of honest broker, negotiating with God on behalf of the people of Cortona. Even the dead in the Lord, with his permission, appeared before Margaret to beg that she chivvy along their living relatives, reminding them to pray for their deceased loved ones, to get them more quickly through the pains of purgatory. The living did not escape her attention either, with Margaret, like Francis in his 'Canticle of the Creatures', advising them to go more frequently to confession. In cases where penitents were insufficiently thorough in their contrition, Margaret would warn them about the sins they had still neglected to confess.

Margaret, for her part, always remained grateful for the spiritual guidance and support of the friars of Cortona. She saw herself as entrusted to them, by the loving words of Christ 'her spouse', who gave her the pet name of 'my little poor one', just as Francis became known as the *poverello* of God. When she founded a hospice for the poor, she continued to help support the friars in their needs also, hopefully without reducing the rations of the non-religious poor:

> To this hospice Margaret gave her heart. And the hospice was made so utterly the poor's own, that in their hour of need Margaret would have nothing spared, either of the movable goods of the house or of the immovable by which she might come generously to their aid. Nor was she unmindful of those who had nurtured her in the spiritual life; for she ordered that out of the food of the said hospice the infirmary of the Friars Minor at Cortona should be fully supplied with whatever was necessary for the sick brethren. Truly was she a Mother of Mercy! But, thoughtful as she was for the needs of other poor, she, who was herself almost penniless, would at no time allow any of the goods of the hospice to be assigned to her own use. (Cuthbert, 1900, p. 90)

Although she lived the latter years of her life as a semi-recluse, Margaret's view of salvation was always of a corporate reality, as was generally true of all medieval Christians. She had become a core member of the town of Cortona and sought the salvation of all through her prayers and her penitential practices. Being Franciscan was for Margaret a matter of being an integral part of the locality in which she lived and, in particular, being a part of the three Orders established by Francis of Assisi. Even though some of the friars thought her consolations to be delusions, and her reputed conversations with Jesus to be fabrications, Margaret always spoke of the Franciscans as her patrons and protectors. Certainly Brother Giunta, and the friars who actively supported her, gave her actions a legitimacy in the eyes of those who doubted her. The historian Mary Harvey Doyno sees the *Life* of Margaret as a testimony to the progressively greater respect in which she was held by both Br Giunta and Ser Badia, the priest at San Basilio. The relationship between Giunta and Margaret was complex and the reader of the text must remember that both had a stake in what was recorded and what was omitted. In the end, it was the people of Cortona that took the lead in seeking official recognition of Margaret's sanctity and her nomination as patron of the town.

Daughter of God, devotee of St Francis

One way in which Margaret entered into the corporate reality of God's presence was through her frequent attendance at the Eucharist. Francis was again her example for this, as he attended a daily Eucharist, which was unusual at the time. There, in the presence of the sacred Host, Margaret vividly experienced Jesus Christ as her loving father:

> And when she had received this most living Bread, which gives life to the world, she heard Jesus Christ sweetly call her his child. Such was the sweetness of his voice that at the sound Margaret was rapt out of herself, and for very joy thought she must die. And in the sweetness of her joy – a joy given to none but those who belong utterly to Christ – she was that day many times raised in ecstasy, becoming unconscious of earthly things, and motionless, as was witnessed by Fra Rainaldo (the Custos), Fra Ubaldo (the Guardian) the lady Gilea, and myself (her confessor).
> And when she came back to her external self, she endeavoured to tell us of what she had experienced as far as she could; but words failed her to express what she had heard and said when absorbed in God, and all she could say was: 'O the immense, the infinite sweetness of God! O day promised me by you, my Lord! O word, full of all gladness, by which you have called me your child!' (Cuthbert, 1900, p. 103)

Here Margaret experiences a kind of out-of-body 'ecstasy', as is described in the stories about Brother Giles of Assisi. Similar experiences are not unknown in most religious traditions, such as the meditative concentration known in the Indian traditions as *samadhi*; during these experiences of deep meditative absorption, the breath and heartbeat can be slowed right down, and pain is not experienced, to the extent that the yogi seems as if dead. The fact that Giunta feels compelled to list the witnesses of the event shows that such phenomena were not met with universal acclaim. Some clearly felt Margaret was pretending to have these conversations with Christ and that she was instead thriving on the attention they brought her. They even tried to validate her ecstasy by getting some women to drag her around by her hair. This was not particularly rough treatment for her day. Other devout women had their ecstasies tested by being pierced with knives or having molten lead poured on their feet. At least Margaret seems to have passed the test without being badly injured. Francis himself is depicted in the early Franciscan texts as going into states of deep absorption in prayer, such as when receiving the stigmata; perhaps this was how he had been able to endure being cauterized for a disease of the eyes without seeming to feel any pain.

Certainly, Margaret felt impelled to imitate Francis in ways that disturbed the friars, who thought her actions too extreme:

The handmaid of Christ had determined for love of her Lord to remedy, if she could, the evil she had done by acts of an opposite nature. She determined therefore to go to Montepulciano, where in former days she had ridden or walked abroad in all the glory of fine clothes, with her face painted and her hair decked out with ornaments of gold, the gifts of her lover. So now she would go, destitute of glory, with her head shaven and clothed in rags. And as she went, she would beg for alms from those in whose midst she had delighted to act the Lady bountiful. She desired, moreover, to take with her a woman who should lead her blindfold with a rope round her neck, and the woman was to cry aloud: 'This, my friends, is Margaret who in the day of her pride did so much evil amongst you.' After this, the woman should publicly cry aloud Margaret's sins as many as could be remembered. (Cuthbert, 1900, pp. 125–6)

Thomas of Celano recounts a similar incident in *The Life of Saint Francis*:

Once, because he was ill, Francis ate a little bit of chicken. When his physical strength returned, he entered the city of Assisi. When he reached the city gate, he commanded the brother who was with him to tie a cord around his neck and drag him through the whole city as if he were a thief, loudly crying out: 'Look! See this glutton who grew fat on the flesh of chickens that he ate without your knowledge.' Many people ran to see this grand spectacle, groaning and weeping ... They were touched in their hearts and were moved to a better way of life by such an example. (*FA:ED*, vol. 1, p. 228)

Margaret had intended that the experience of public humiliation would allow her to identify with the Christ who was scorned and mocked by the crowds at his death. But her confessor Giunta would have none of it. He counselled discretion, pointing out that sometimes self-contempt can actually increase one's pride, and therefore forbade her to attempt to fulfil her plan. Even if Francis could get away with such things, being able to command his companion to take part in the scheme, Margaret was well advised not to employ such drastic measures. Being Franciscan didn't mean imitating Francis in all that he did. It was enough to confess one's sins to a priest, not to the whole town. In this way Margaret could avoid the risk of compounding her failings, while at the same time developing the virtue of obedience.

On another occasion, Margaret had the idea that she should mutilate her face, albeit not so badly that it would risk her death. For some reason she felt that her natural beauty was a hindrance to her faith. Perhaps she didn't want to be distracted from the path of humility by the admiration of others; or maybe she resented being labelled as an object of desire when her only wish was to be the beloved spouse of her God. Most likely she had internalized the pervasive oppression of women in medieval society, justified by the perception of them as the tempters of men and the cause of the Fall. In any case, Giunta vehemently forbade such drastic action, saying that if she went ahead with it, he would have nothing more to do with her. Perhaps, in both examples, the mere fact that she asked his permission suggests that she was just feeling her way, wanting to release the pent-up feelings of inadequacy and self-loathing that plagued her. This tendency to self-harm, often expressed in excessive abstinence from food or drink, or the infliction of pain by the wearing of coarse penitential clothing, is one of the more troubling aspects of medieval spirituality. Mostly it was women who succumbed to this darker side of religion, though some men, like Francis and before him Bernard of Clairvaux, were not immune to the temptation to treat their bodies with contempt. At least Francis could say at the end of his life that he apologized to 'Brother Ass' – that is his body – for not having treated it with more respect (see *FA:ED*, vol. 2, pp. 235, 383).

Margaret was greatly devoted to Francis, wanting to imitate him, and finding in him the father-figure she seems never to have found in her family life. She craved the parental approval of God and of the friars of Cortona and found in them the security she had lost when her lover was killed. In another of her dialogues with the Lord, she talks about her appreciation of Francis:

Now this loving daughter, hearing the Lord utter the name of her father St Francis, at once said: 'O great and powerful Lord, much did you love my father St Francis, for with great gifts you honoured him.' And the Lord said: 'Much in truth did I love him, and much was I loved by him, and I tell you it is very sweet to me when people love his Order, because of him whom I have loved in all sweetness. Therefore do not be concerned because your companion rebuked you because you said in an excess of admiration that your father St Francis was as a new god: for in some ways I have made him like to me.' (Cuthbert, 1900, p. 153)

Veneration of Francis, even during his life, acclaimed him not just as a saint but as an *alter Christus*, another Christ. A massive fourteenth-century tome, called *The Book of the Conformity* by Bartholomew of Pisa, catalogued the many parallels between the lives of Francis and Jesus Christ. Margaret did not go so far in her own devotion to Francis, but she certainly found inspiration in the life of the saint of Assisi and found meaning in her own life as a disciple of Francis.

Learning the spiritual disciplines

One way Margaret expressed her devotion to her Lord was by her use of the spiritual discipline of fasting:

Margaret, the servant of the Lord, most eager out of her love for Christ for every discipline of her body, spurned all kinds of tasty food. After her conversion, for the rest of her life she did not want to eat fresh figs because when she lived in the world she was very fond of them. She declared this standard: that even were she to be quite weak, she would not eat the flesh of birds or of four-footed beasts ... she maintained her frail body just on bread, raw greens, a few hazelnuts, or perhaps some almonds. Before meals she would offer lengthy prayers along with groans and deep sighs, and afterwards, when she would give thanks, inviting all saints and creatures to join her in the praise of our providential Lord. She would never try to eat a meal unless she first said the divine office, or at least said five *Pater nosters* along with five salutations of the blessed Virgin, in memory of the five wounds of Jesus Christ. After the meal was finished she would offer the same number of *Pater nosters*. (Bevegnati, 2012, p. 78)

Margaret clearly struggled with her appetite. Her scribe says it was 'out of love for Christ', and one hopes that it was so. The Christian practice of fasting was in part based on an identification with Jesus fasting in the wilderness and battling with the devil's temptations, as recorded in the Gospels. The first Christian monastics, known as the desert fathers and mothers, saw 'concupiscence', desire in general, and gluttony and lust in particular, as being among the chief thoughts that plague anyone seeking to still the restless mind as a precursor to contemplative prayer. These were practical rather than abstract teachings by monks such as Evagrius and his disciple John Cassian, whose works were recommended by Benedict in his Rule. In later medieval piety in the Western Church, the concentration on the eucharistic bread as the sole food necessary for maintenance of both body and soul was not unknown.

As to Margaret's own practice of fasting, her rule was to have as plain a diet as possible. It seems a shame that she refused to eat fresh figs simply because she used to like them before her conversion. At least that is Giunta's understanding; perhaps Margaret found figs a troubling aphrodisiac. She seems to have settled on a vegan diet as most helpful to her ascetic practice, not unlike Mahatma Gandhi, who spent most of his auto-biography (*The Story of my Experiments with Truth*) talking about diet and celibacy rather than politics. In Margaret's day, not eating meat was a common religious practice in Western Christendom: Benedict's Rule (chapter 39) legislates against it, though it was allowed to build up the strength of sick monks and nuns, and poultry or fish were usually deemed acceptable for all. Fasting, such as during Lent, implied an abstinence from animal products for all Christians, hence the using up of eggs on Shrove Tuesday in the tradition of serving pancakes. Fasting on nothing more than bread and water was the domain of only hardened ascetics and was used as a punishment for recalcitrant religious. Most often, extreme fasting was associated with female ascetics. Carolyn Walker Bynum (1987) and other historians of the Middle Ages have pointed out how the intake of food was one of the few areas in which medieval women had control over their lives. Perhaps Margaret was using the meal table as her laboratory of the spirit, seeing the effect of different foods on the mind, and finding ways to enhance her sense of the immanent presence of God. Some scholars, such as Rudolph Bell (1985), have described the more extreme fasting practices of medieval saints as a kind of 'holy anorexia', denying themselves adequate nutrition so as to preserve the purity of their souls rather than the slimness of their physique. Both secular and sacred versions of this condition can be accompanied by an exaggerated sense of transgression, whether of the norms of perceived beauty or of the requirements of an unattainable sinlessness.

Whatever Margaret allowed on the meal table, it can't have taken long to consume. Probably the prayers before and after eating took longer than the meal itself. Reciting the Lord's Prayer (the *Pater noster*) was the staple diet of Margaret's practice of prayer, as were the Hail Mary and other prayers in honour of the Blessed Virgin Mary. If anything, her prayers seem too scrupulous, such that her confessor had to reassure her that she needn't be so prolix in her praying:

> Margaret was so anxious to please the Most High that she never ceased to cry over some supposed sin of negligence, even though in fact she had not committed any. She considered herself lacking in virtue if she did not contemplate God, practise austerities, help her neighbours, put up with her infirmities, and recite every day at least 600 Our Fathers, Hail Marys and Doxologies.
>
> To ease her sorrow and mitigate her inconsolable tears, I explained to her that her ardent desire for Christ and her assiduous meditation on his Passion are in effect a form of perpetual prayer. I assured her that mental prayer is more delightful and efficacious than vocal prayer. (Bevegnati, 2012, p. 111)

It is perhaps no wonder that some of her Franciscan fathers looked askance at her religiosity. She was beating them at their

own game, being more religious than the religious. Giunta
and Christ, acting as her two confessors, spend a lot of time
responding to Margaret's scruples about sin. No doubt, like
many confessors, they often reassure her that she is not as bad
as she thinks. God doesn't require such hours spent in vocal
prayer, they tell her: God looks on the habitual state of the
heart, not on the frequency of prayers recited from books.
Nonetheless, Margaret sets her own goals and is undeniably
thorough in her prayers, particularly in her almost constant
recitation of the *Pater noster*, the Lord's Prayer:

> Now the more she pondered on the benefits which Christ
> has bestowed upon the human race, the more fervently did
> Margaret pray for souls. She was accustomed to keep count
> in her prayers by a measure of beans which she put into
> a small vase, taking out a bean at each *pater* in this way,
> namely; in reparation for her own sins, which she deplored
> bitterly, she would say four hundred *paters*; for the Order
> of St Francis, one hundred *paters*; for the elect who were in
> a state of grace, one hundred *paters*; for sinners disrobed of
> grace, one hundred *paters*; for her confessor, one hundred
> *paters*; for the delivery of the Holy Land from the Saracens,
> one hundred *paters*; for those who did homage to the Mother
> of God, one hundred *paters*; for the children she held at the
> font and their godfathers, one hundred *paters*; for the people
> of Cortona who were kind to her, one hundred *paters*; and
> for those who did her injury, one hundred *paters*.
>
> Thus Margaret, having given her heart to God to watch
> with him, was unable to repress the fire of divine love which
> made her open out her heart to all humankind. With all care
> she continued to study how best to assist her neighbours with
> the means within her power, now speaking for them in her
> colloquies with God, now bringing them temporal assistance,
> and now pouring forth her prayers for them. (Cuthbert,
> 1900, pp. 219–20)

Surprisingly, Margaret doesn't use a rosary to count her prayers, being content with moving beans back and forth from a jar. Strings of beads used to count prayers were originally called *Pater nosters* as they were used to recite the Our Father, that is, the Lord's Prayer. One circuit of 50 recitations repeated three times was treated as equivalent to the recitation of all 150 psalms of the psalter, for those unable to read. Dominican tradition suggests that the modern form of the rosary was given to St Dominic, the contemporary of St Francis and founder of the Order of Preachers, early in the thirteenth century. It would therefore have been quite a modern devotion at the time of Margaret. Probably there were earlier versions of this devotion, but there is no clear documentary evidence of their use until later in the fifteenth century, when it was promoted by the Dominican priest and theologian Alanus de Rupe. Presumably if there had been rosary beads to hand, Margaret would have used them. In the Orthodox Church, Anthony the Great and Pachomius, founders of Egyptian Christian monasticism in the fourth century, are credited with inventing the prayer rope for counting prayers and prostrations.

Margaret was clearly a devoted practitioner of this form of almost continuous prayer. Repeating biblical phrases in prayer goes back to the earliest desert monastics, who used exclamations from the psalms such as, 'O God make speed to save me; O Lord, make haste to help me!' (Ps. 70.1) The Jesus Prayer, 'Lord Jesus Christ, Son of God, have mercy on me a sinner!' became particularly associated with the Eastern Orthodox Church and has remained a popular devotion to this day. Perhaps Jesus himself prayed using repeated phrases from the psalms, or the individual petitions of the prayer known to us as the Lord's Prayer, or perhaps he simply breathed the ancient name of God indicated by the Hebrew consonants YHWH.

The list of those Margaret prayed for gives an insight into how she used these prayers. Rather than being a simple act of worship, these were largely intercessory prayers, both for her friends and for her enemies. In effect she is listing all the people she would have come across in her daily life, as well as all those she remembered from the past. This repetition would have moulded her thoughts into a perpetual wish for the good of anyone coming into her orbit. It was above all a formation in compassion, a desire for the blessing of anyone in need.

Enacting the gospel

But her prayers didn't end with intercessory lists. Giunta's book continues for several pages listing all the biblical events she then goes on to remember, just as in the evocation of the 'mysteries' in a modern rosary. In this way she would have contemplated the events of the life of Jesus, from the womb to the grave and beyond, imagining herself into scenes such as the Annunciation, the Visitation, the Nativity and so on, feeling the appropriate emotions of joy or sorrow. Above all, she pored over the events of the final week of the life of Jesus, weeping and crying out, totally absorbed in the sorrowful mysteries unfolding before her inward eyes.

It was Margaret's custom every day of the week to make the Stations of the Cross; yet in a special manner these sacred mysteries renewed themselves in her heart on Fridays, on which day, she would say, she could not understand how any Christian could be merry; and on Good Friday she was like a mother who had lost her son.

Now one Good Friday in the depths of her anguish she cut off her hair and ran to the church of the Friars, and she would thus have gone to the other churches but her sense of what was fitting restrained her. Then, as she was weeping over the Passion, the Divine Redeemer spoke to her: 'Margaret, if you were in a deep, woody solitude on a dark night surrounded by all manner of dangers, would you hesitate to come to me?' To which Margaret replied at once: 'My Lord, I believe I should be like a little child who, hearing its mother's voice, runs to her at once and falls and rises again quickly and runs again.' (Cuthbert, 1900, pp. 192–3)

Meditating on the Stations of the Cross became one of the characteristic devotions of the Franciscans. As custodians of many of the shrines in the Holy Land, the Franciscans actively encouraged pilgrimage to the sacred sites. But not everyone could afford the travelling expenses or risk the dangers of the road, so representative shrines were established in friaries to enable people to make the journey at one remove. This is one of the earliest references to such a devotional practice.

Margaret, of course, enters into the devotion with gusto, but is not totally out of control in these situations. She still exhibits an admirable 'sense of what was fitting'. She knows the limits of what the people of Cortona will find acceptable and is sensible enough not to risk being ostracized as out of her mind. What she seems to be doing is as much theatrical as theological. Just as Francis created a crib scene one Christmas at Greccio, so that everyone could feel they were there for the first Christmas Day, so Margaret recreated Holy Week on the streets and in the churches of Cortona, so that everyone could participate by their groans and their tears.

Sometimes this led to a total identification with one of the characters, such as Mary Magdalene searching for the crucified Jesus:

Full of love for Christ, she used to say: 'Have you seen my Lord? Where can I, who am most wretched, find him? ... Why have you abandoned me, my love? Why do you hide from me? ...' Throughout this state of anxiety, which lasted until the morning of the following Sunday, Margaret did not eat or sleep. On the following Sunday, when Mass was being celebrated and I was preaching from the pulpit in the church of the Friars Minor, Margaret, being ashamed and fearful, could not restrain her impulses of sorrow. In front of everyone, she began shouting like someone out of her mind, and asked me if I knew where the crucified Lord was, and where I had taken him. At seeing Margaret in such a state, all the men and women present broke down and cried, so moved were they with fervent devotion. Then she turned to me for assurance that she would find her teacher. Without interrupting my sermon on the word of God, I answered in a loud voice that the Saviour, whom she so ardently sought, in his kindness and generosity would cease to conceal himself from her and would soon make his presence known. After she heard this, Margaret, who was ghostly pale, sat down in the sight of all. (Bevegnati, 2012, pp. 109–10)

With her acute sense of sin, Margaret easily identified with the Magdalene, who was portrayed in the Middle Ages as a penitent sinner, using the story of Mary of Bethany in the Gospel of Luke, who with great love and many tears washed the feet of Jesus. Giunta had to speak to Margaret 'in a loud voice' to stop her totally distracting the Sunday congregation from the sermon he was preaching, but really it was Margaret who was enacting the sermon, telling the gospel with the tears of her distress.

For Margaret, these re-enactments of biblical themes were her way of studying the Scriptures. Indeed, she loved to hear the Bible read:

> Now Margaret was ever desirous of hearing the word of God, and this truly is a sign of grace. She was never so weak, never so destitute of energy, but, listening to her confessor speaking of divine things, her soul would be filled at once with joy. And as a garden well-cultivated and rich in soil she would receive the seed of the divine word. She would sometimes say to her confessor: 'Fra Giunta, father of my soul, speak to me of God, for the divine word gladdens and inflames my spirit, illumines and comforts it, and at the same time heals my body; for so long as that word sounds in my soul, I feel nothing of my bodily infirmities.' (Cuthbert, 1900, pp. 216–17)

In this respect she was like Francis, who steeped himself in the Scriptures, particularly the psalms. As a token of his devotion to the Passion of Christ he wrote an *Office of the Passion*. This was a sequence of psalms adapted to give the impression of being prayed by Jesus, linked with the hours of the last day of his life. Recited by heart after the end of the regular daily office, these prayers centred Francis on the self-offering of Jesus.

Pray continually

Margaret was continually recollecting herself in the presence of Christ, often simply focusing on his name:

> Moreover, she carried the name of Jesus ever in her heart, and whenever it came into her speech she was filled with a great tenderness. She would exclaim: 'O Name sweet above all names; Name of him by whose power I was recalled to grace, by whose Blood I was redeemed; whose love of me has drawn me to love only him!' (Cuthbert, 1900, p. 217)

Both Francis and Margaret were devoted to Jesus, his mother and the holy angels as protectors of their faith. As part of the Office of the Passion, Francis wrote a prayer to Mary, to be used as an antiphon after each psalm. This meant that it would have been recited 14 times a day as part of this private devotion:

> Holy Virgin Mary,
> among the women born into the world,
> there is no one like you.
> Daughter and servant
> of the most high and supreme King
> and of the Father in heaven,
> Mother of our most holy Lord Jesus Christ,
> Spouse of the Holy Spirit,
> pray for us
> with Saint Michael the Archangel,
> all the powers of heaven
> and all the saints,

at the side of your most holy beloved Son,
our Lord and Teacher.
Glory to the Father, and to the Son, and to the Holy Spirit.
As it was in the beginning, is now, and will be forever. Amen.
(*FA:ED*, vol. 1, p. 141)

Repeating these words so many times a day must have deeply formed the faith of Francis. Clare also memorized the *Office of the Passion* and no doubt found it reinforced her own devotion to Jesus her spouse. The opening greeting: 'Holy Virgin Mary, among the women born into the world, there is no one like you' is not without its difficulties. Feminist theologians have pointed out the criticism that this designation is impossible for women to emulate: how can one be both virgin and mother? And if only Mary is able to attain this, does that not leave all other women as obstacles on the path of salvation, denizens of the flesh rather than guides in the ascent to the heavenly realms?

In the Franciscan tradition, at least, there are mitigating factors in this form of devotion. Mary may indeed be daughter of her heavenly father, mother of Jesus and spouse of the Holy Spirit, but so are all those who do penance in this world. Francis wrote in his *Later Admonition and Exhortation to the Brothers and Sisters of Penance* that all men and women can be spouses, brothers and mothers of the Lord Jesus Christ:

We are spouses when the faithful soul is united by the Holy Spirit to our Lord Jesus Christ. We are brothers, moreover, when we do the will of his Father who is in heaven; mothers when we carry him in our heart and body through love and a pure and sincere conscience; and give him birth through a holy activity, which must shine before others by example. (*FA:ED*, vol. 1, p. 149)

All Christians can share in the brotherhood of Christ and the motherhood of Mary. All, men and women, are spouses of the Holy Spirit. Certainly, Margaret was devoted to the mother of Jesus:

One day, after she had devoutly received the Body of our Lord, Margaret heard him say: 'Daughter, servant of God, praise and honour my mother, who is so beautiful and pure. Neither the world nor the scriptures speak of her excellence and splendour. I have made her in my highest and best eternal wisdom as my mother and lady.' (Bevegnati, 2012, p. 153)

As well as having a vivid devotion to Mary, Margaret rejoices in the company of angels:

On the night of the feast of the virgin St Clare when Margaret was praying in her cell an angel with six wings appeared to her. His blessing felt like a furnace of love and filled her with such interior bliss that she could not restrain from laughing. During the night the angel descended to her several times and renewed this sense of joy. (Bevegnati, 2012, p. 168)

And yet it was not all sweetness and light for Margaret. There is great rejoicing in the presence of God and the angels and saints, but there is also the desert of the spiritual life:

Margaret exclaimed: 'Truly you are my Father, my Awakener, my Spouse, my Gladness, Joy of all joys!' And the Lord made answer: 'And you are my child, my companion, my chosen one.' Then said Margaret: 'Lord, send me not back into the desert.' The Lord replied: 'I send you back even as a sheep amongst wolves.' Margaret exclaimed: 'My Lord, let this citadel of my body be quickly destroyed that through the ruins I may pass to you.' But the Lord: 'And yet no suffering is so bitter to you as to be without me.' Margaret: 'You are indeed, Lord, my very life, through whom I live. If you send me back into the desert I shall die. You are my treasure; without you all wealth is to me but direst poverty.' But Christ told her she must indeed go back into the desert; yet, while he said this, he showed himself to her, smiling sweetly upon her. (Cuthbert, 1900, pp. 222–3)

The three classic stages of the spiritual life, beloved of Bonaventure, and a frequent theme in spiritual texts since at least

Dionysius in the sixth century – purgation, illumination and union – are not sequential for Margaret but rather cyclical. The experience of the desert is a purification of the exuberance she feels at other times. Often her visions are like love letters from the Lord, but there are times of darkness too. Questions have to be asked about her emotional stability: was she perhaps suffering from a bipolar condition? Were her tears and smiles influenced by the chemistry of her brain? To which the only answer can be: of course they were! But so are all people as long as they are embodied. (And if the resurrection of the body is a reality, then when are we not embodied beings in some form or another?) At the end of the day, Margaret is to be celebrated because she navigates the stormy waters of her emotional vibrancy with such infectious passion and joy. She may be a round-the-world yachtswoman being blown this way and that by a thousand storms, but at the end she reaches the harbour, and with her Lord, she comes home:

> Having tasted the divine sweetness, Margaret, her face glowing with serenity and joy, exclaimed with an angelic smile: 'The Lord has prepared this day for me to become inebriated with the pleasure of divine love.' She remained this way motionless and with eyes wide open, but not seeing anything. Then the Lord spoke to her heart and asked her how much her soul had expanded on this day. She responded: 'Lord, my soul is now greater than the whole world, because I have you within me; heaven and earth together cannot contain you.' (Bevegnati, 2012, p. 177)

A passionate Passion

To end this chapter, I offer a story of the Passion of Jesus and his servant and lover, Margaret:

> It was in the consideration of the Passion of the Heavenly King and of the sorrow which it brought his Virgin mother

that Margaret found strength to suffer gladly and without effort. Now, one night in prayer she besought the Lord of his goodness to grant her to feel, as far as she was able, something of the sorrow which pierced the heart of his Mother standing beside the Cross; nor would she be denied. Then did she hear Christ say to her: 'At sunrise you shall go as usual to the church of my Friars, and there the scenes of my Passion shall be brought before you, and you shall experience at the sight such anguish and bitterness and pain as you have never yet known or felt.'

She came therefore to the church at the stated hour and humbly asked for me, her confessor and unworthy servant, and as a special favour begged me on no account to leave the church, as it had been revealed to her that she would that day be crucified in spirit with Christ on the cross.

The Mass was over, and it was near the third hour of the morning, when this devoted soul, becoming absorbed in God, began to drink the vinegar of the Passion. She saw Christ betrayed in the Garden; ... she beheld the merciless scourging at the pillar, and saw Christ mocked, blindfolded, and spat upon; ... And from time to time as Margaret beheld this mystery of the Passion, she would exclaim: 'Now he is brought forth from the palace!' 'Now he is being taken out of the gate!' 'Now Simon is forced to help him!' 'Now they are putting the thieves one on each side of my Lord!' and so forth till the end.

The sight of Margaret thus rapt in the contemplation of the passion so stirred the inhabitants of Cortona, and so moved them to pity, that many times that day men and women left their work or employment – they even left babes in their cradles and the sick in their beds – to come and see Margaret, so that the oratory resounded with their sobs. For it seemed to them that Margaret was not beside the cross but upon it, suffering cruel pains. Indeed such marks of suffering appeared in her that we might well have thought her to be in the very agony of death. She clenched her teeth; her face became discoloured and her pulse ceased to beat. She was unable to speak and became quite cold. Even when she returned to herself she could hardly make herself understood, so hoarse was her voice. At the ninth hour she became insensible and lost her sight, so that she was not aware of the crowds of people around her, nor could she distinguish the voices or faces of the ladies who were attending her. And since I do not wish to pass over anything which happened that day, I will tell you how when the ninth hour arrived, the hour when the Saviour, bowing his head, gave up the ghost, Margaret also bowed her head sideways till it rested on her bosom; and the people seeing her without motion or sensibility thought her dead. And so she remained until evening, shedding no tear. But when evening came she rose up as it were from the dead and lifted up her face now suffused with the renewed joy of her mind, and gazing upwards with eyes of gladness towards the heavens as one who had received some new and wonderful gift, she gave thanks to God the giver of all good things. When, however, she turned around and saw the crowd of people a bitter fear took the place of her great joy, and she began to be troubled in spirit because of the presence of the people. But he, the desired Lover, set her fears at rest, speaking to her and saying: 'Be not afraid and have no scruple concerning whatsoever has been done in you this day; for I have made you to be a mirror for sinners, even the most obstinate, that through you they may learn how freely my mercy is opened out to them that they may be saved.' Hearing these words, Margaret was grateful to God; and being solicitous of her neighbour, she replied: 'Most high God! Willingly will I remain here or wheresoever you will, if so I may be made an occasion of glory to you or of salvation to the people whom you have redeemed.'

Then turning to us who were marvelling at this sudden revival of her bodily powers, she said that she felt stronger now than in the early morning before she had entered into the passion. (Cuthbert, 1900, pp. 176–81)

5

The Scholar: Bonaventure of Bagnoregio (1217/21–1274)

Francis of Assisi was not a scholar. He could read and write passable Latin, which was the language used for nearly every written document across Europe in his day, but he was not a keen student. The study of theology was, after all, the preserve of university-educated clerics. As the son of a merchant, Francis would have known what was necessary for his father's business, how to draw up a bill and so on, but he had little formal education. He would have been taught by a priest who was probably only just literate himself. In his day, notaries were generally commissioned to draw up Latin documents. The very few examples of his own handwriting still in existence show a number of grammatical mistakes, with corrections made by his friend and secretary, Brother Leo. Francis was, however, something of a poet, as seen by his *Earlier Rule* with its long, flowing exhortations, or his famous 'Canticle of the Creatures', the latter being composed in his native Umbrian dialect. But his writings comprise little more than some letters and prayers, his *Testament* and the *Rule* finally approved after the cardinal given responsibility for the Order had sifted through it. Francis did engage with current church teaching, for example regarding the Eucharist, which he included in some of his letters, but it is difficult to tell exactly how much was his own composition and how much he owed to the skill of those who helped him as a scribe.

Francis was not unintelligent: by all accounts he had a good memory and was able to learn large sections of Scripture by heart, particularly from the Gospels and the psalms. In fact, it was normal in those days for monastics to memorize the psalms as they would be chanted frequently in chapel with little lighting, with the antiphons, the refrains, written out in elaborate antiphonals for the use of cantors at a central lectern. There are even illustrations in medieval texts contrasting Franciscans and Dominicans not just by the colour of their habits but by the presence or absence of prayer books in their hands: the Franciscans being portrayed as so poor that their hands were empty, though their hearts were full of praise. Despite their tendency to try to minimize the use of books, the Franciscans were instrumental in the development of shortened prayer books known as breviaries. They were often on the road, preaching and teaching wherever a pulpit was made available, or a market crowd was willing to be distracted from their shopping by the entertainment of a sermon. Franciscans needed to be able to say their prayers on the go. You could say that they were the first users of a pocket prayer book, simplifying the daily prayers, the Office or 'Hours', and enabling their use when travelling. Much later, at the time of the Reformation, it was a Franciscan Office book that Thomas Cranmer chiefly used as a model for his own much-abbreviated Book of Common Prayer.

Francis was keen to always have a brother companion so that he could say the Daily Office, with its versicles and responses, spread out through the day and night. These were important times to reconnect with the Word of God through the words of the Holy Scriptures. Even if it was pouring with rain he would stop and say his prayers – another good reason for being able to recite the prayers by heart while keeping the book itself safely dry. But Francis hated the idea of his brothers becoming proud of their linguistic accomplishments. Concerning these issues, the *Later Rule* of 1223 states: 'Let those who are illiterate not be anxious to learn, but let them pay attention to what they must desire above all else: to have the Spirit of the Lord and its holy activity, to pray always to him with a pure heart' (*FA:ED*, vol. 1, p. 105). These prayers, for the illiterate brothers, would consist largely of repetitions of the Lord's Prayer. A pure heart was enough: an educated mind able to read and find the right page in a prayer book (never an easy task), was not essential.

'I, a breviary'

Not all the brothers saw things in quite the same way, as recounted in the following episode from *The Assisi Compilation*:

There was once a brother novice who could read the psalter, but not very well. And because he enjoyed reading, he sought permission from the general minister to have a psalter and the minister granted it to him. But he did not wish to have it unless he first had permission from blessed Francis, especially since he had heard that blessed Francis did not want his brothers to be desirous of learning and books ...

And blessed Francis told him: 'After you have a psalter, you will desire and want to have a breviary; after you have a breviary, you will sit in a fancy chair, like a great prelate telling your brother: "Bring me the breviary."' And speaking in this way with great intensity of spirit, he took some ashes in his hand, put them on his head rubbing them around his head as though he were washing it, saying: 'I, a breviary! I, a breviary!' He spoke this way many times, passing his hand over his head. The brother was stunned and ashamed.

Afterwards blessed Francis said to him: 'Brother, I was likewise tempted to have books. But, in order to know God's will about this, I took the book, where the Lord's Gospels are written, and prayed to the Lord to deign to show it to me at the first opening of the book. After my prayer was ended, on the first opening of the holy Gospel this verse of the holy Gospel came to me: *To you it is given to know the mystery of the kingdom of God, but to the others all things are treated in parables*' (Mark 4.11).

And he said: 'There are many who willingly climb to the

heights of knowledge; that person be blessed who renounces it for the love of God.' (*FA:ED*, vol. 2, pp. 207–9)

The sentence that always surprises me in this quotation is where Francis says to the novice, 'Brother, I was likewise tempted to have books.' Really? He doesn't come across as being keen to do much study, but here he seems to be saying that he consciously renounced 'the heights of knowledge' for the sake of the love of God. Francis certainly loved to travel and to learn new things. If he wrote *The Admonitions* attributed to him, with their allusions to scholarly theological writings, then perhaps he did call in to friary and monastic libraries on his wanderings around Italy. Indeed, he once wrote a letter to his brother Anthony of Padua, a renowned theologian and gifted preacher:

Brother Francis sends greetings to Brother Anthony, my Bishop.
I am pleased that you teach sacred theology to the brothers providing that, as is contained in the Rule, you 'do not extinguish the Spirit of prayer and devotion' during study of this kind. (*FA:ED*, vol. 1, p. 107)

It was pride and haughtiness that Francis abhorred, not study itself. He always wanted his community to be made of Lesser Brothers, not greater prelates or professors. Anything that undermined the simplicity of the Order was a challenge to its whole ethos. And if owning a book, even a prayer book, took away that sense of humility, then it had to go. Knowledge (*scientia*) had to be renounced if it undermined wisdom (*sapientia*).

This is where the Franciscan friar Bonaventure steps in, to show Franciscans how to reconcile knowledge with understanding, holding in balance and treasuring both science and wisdom. For Bonaventure, following in the footprints of Francis, theology was a form of wisdom because it perfects the mind through the affections: devotion is the basis of doctrine. As

Bonaventure says in the Prologue to his *Commentary on the Sentences of Peter Lombard*:

> The intellect ... is perfected by a habit that lies between the purely speculative and the purely practical, but one that embraces both. This habit is called wisdom and it involves knowledge and affection together: 'For the wisdom of doctrine is like her name' (Ecclus. 6.22, Vulgate translation). Consequently, this habit is for the sake of contemplation and also for our becoming good, but principally for the sake of our becoming good. (Bonaventure, 2013, p. 83)

When combined with the teaching Bonaventure gives in *Hexaemeron* 19.3, written in 1273 towards the end of his life, we see the progression: faith → science / knowledge → contemplation → moral perfection / sanctity → wisdom. Or in other words, for the Franciscan, we can only be wise if we combine knowledge with affection; simple contemplation of reality is incomplete without the love that leads to wisdom.

Such an understanding of wisdom helped Bonaventure later when he was Minister General of the Order of Friars Minor and trying to hold together two extremes among the brethren. Some, later known as 'Spirituals', tended to want to go straight from faith to sanctity and wisdom; others, the 'Conventuals' could get stuck at the level of science without developing the moral perfection leading to wisdom (see Bonaventure, 2013, p. 92, n. 42). For Bonaventure, science, or knowledge, had to be developed along with sanctity, thus justifying the study of the arts and sciences, including the teaching of the ancient Greek philosophers Plato and Aristotle. In this way, the true scholar could 'plunder the Egyptians' (Ex. 12.36) as the Israelites did on their escape from captivity; the riches of knowledge could legitimately be brought into use in the service of the gospel.

Books and other tools

Bonaventure of Bagnoregio was a very keen scholar. Born in
1217 or 21, as a teenager he was sent to the University of Paris,
the most prestigious centre of learning of the day. There he was
recognized as an exceptionally bright student, with a purity
of heart and a warm devotion to Christ that made him far
from being a dry academic. At this stage he was still in secular
garb and continued as such until he had completed his Master
of Arts degree. It was while studying at Paris that he became
familiar with the Order of Friars Minor, sitting at the feet of the
first Franciscan Theology masters, Alexander of Hales (1185–
1245), John of La Rochelle (1200–1245) and Odo Rigaldus
(1200–1275). There he himself joined the Franciscans, taking
the name Brother Bonaventure in place of his baptismal name
John. After completing his studies, producing commentaries
on the Gospel of Luke and the *Sentences* of Peter Lombard,
Bonaventure was appointed Master of the Franciscan school
at Paris in 1253.

Bonaventure would have loved books: the smell of them,
their sturdy weight in the hand and the pleasures of the
heavenly realms to which they carried him. He believed that
to fulfil their calling by God as friars it was essential that at
least some of the brothers should study and become learned
in the disciplines of theology. In *A Letter in Response to an
Unknown Master*, Bonaventure mounts a defence against
those who would criticize the scholarly direction in which the
Order was turning:

> Hear me now on what I have to say about books and other
> tools. The Rule states in no uncertain terms that the brothers
> have the right and duty of preaching, something that, to my
> knowledge, is found in no other religious rule. Now, if they
> are not to preach fables but the divine Word, which they
> cannot know unless they read, nor read unless they have
> books, then it is perfectly clear that it is totally in harmony
> with the perfection of the Rule for them to have books, just

as it is for them to preach. Furthermore, if it's not harmful to the poverty of the Order to have missals for celebrating Mass and breviaries for reciting the Hours, then it is not detrimental to have books and Bibles for preaching the divine Word. The brothers are therefore allowed to have books. (Bonaventure, 1994, p. 46)

Bonaventure begins this section of his letter by referring to 'books and other tools'. This may be an allusion to the *Earlier Rule* of St Francis where he states that 'it is lawful for [the brothers] to have the tools and instruments for their trades' (*FA:ED*, vol. 1, p. 69), providing they receive only what they need, such as food or clothing, but not money. This vision of honest manual work inspired Francis to the end, writing in his *Testament*: 'I worked with my hands, and I still desire to work; and I earnestly desire all brothers to give themselves to honest work ... for example and to avoid idleness' (*FA:ED*, vol. 1, p. 125).

Writing some 28 years after the death of Francis, Bonaventure had to be a little creative in his interpretation of the founder's teaching on the work of study, pointing out that the *Later Rule* of 1223, the one officially approved by the pope, slightly shifts the emphasis, talking about 'those brothers to whom the Lord has given the grace of working' (*FA:ED*, vol. 1, p. 102). So it depends on the gift and calling of grace, in other words on the desire of the individual brother as led by the Spirit to do manual work, rather than being essential for all. Bonaventure goes on to gently challenge the example of Francis, saying: 'Although [Francis] was the most perfect observer of the Rule, I do not believe that by his own hands he ever earned so much as twelve pence or their equivalent. Instead, he greatly admonished the brothers to prayerfulness' (Bonaventure, 1994, p. 50).

But Bonaventure is in basic agreement with Francis. In his *Salutation of the Virtues*, Francis began: 'Hail Queen Wisdom! May the Lord protect you, with your Sister, holy pure Simplicity!' (*FA:ED*, vol. 1, p. 164) For Francis, the virtue of simplicity, able to confound 'all the wisdom of this world', was most clearly seen in the simple, uneducated brothers. But Queen Wisdom and humble Simplicity are sisters, not competitors; both are foundational virtues in the religious life. Academic work and manual work are both legitimate ways of Franciscan service, each requiring their own particular skills and tools. And in all of Bonaventure's writings, the ideals of true wisdom and the spirit of prayerfulness are prized and praised, as we shall see later in this chapter.

So far, so good; the community's library budget is saved. The brothers are being asked to preach and to say their prayers, so they need Bibles and prayer books, and commentaries and liturgical books, and books of doctrine and spirituality. But is there a more fundamental issue at stake here, a principle that goes to the heart of what it means to be Franciscan? Bonaventure continues his defence:

> But then doesn't the Rule contradict itself, for in another section it commands the brothers not to have anything? God forbid that there should be any contradiction in it, just as there is no error, since it is completely drawn from the wellsprings of the Gospel, as is easy for me to show. On this point, I maintain that the use of these things is permitted the friars; it is the ownership that is forbidden. For the rule does not demand that brothers should not 'have' anything or 'use' anything, which would be insane, but rather, that 'they should not acquire anything as their own.' Well then, who does own the things that the brothers are using? My answer is: that to whomever they belong, they are neither mine nor the Order's; and that's enough to satisfy the purity of my conscience. (Bonaventure, 1994, pp. 46–7)

After talking about 'books and other tools' used for study, Bonaventure is met by another objection: studying books may be necessary for the work of preaching, but what about the vow of poverty? Books were expensive, luxury items at that time, laboriously copied out by hand by monks or professional scribes in cold scriptoria, bent over their desks in the gloom of guttering candlelight. How could a Franciscan friar be poor when he had a well-stocked library in his convent and a shelf full of books in his own room, if he had one, or in his cubicle in a shared dormitory?

Here Bonaventure draws the distinction between ownership and use. Of course the friars may use books, he says, but that doesn't mean they are their personal possessions. So who do they belong to? He can't say that they belong to the Order because that would be a violation of the corporate poverty that the Order bound itself to maintain. In the end, the problem was solved in two ways. First Bonaventure says that the books and other essential items given to the friars still in some way belong to the donors, even if they are sitting on conventual shelves. They are given in the knowledge that, technically, they can be taken back if the friars do not live up to their calling. And in any case, they are received by an 'agent' rather than the friars themselves; the friars are spared the reception or use of money, or the handling of gifts. All this was stipulated in the document *Quo elongati* (1230) issued by Pope Gregory IX just four years after the death of his great friend Francis of Assisi. But ultimately the problem was resolved by Pope Innocent IV, declaring in *Ordinem Vestrum* (1245) that he was the actual owner of all the Franciscans' property which he was merely lending to the friars. In this way they would be released from concerns about material support, so that they could concentrate on study so as to avoid preaching heresy or misleading the conscience of penitents making their confession of sins.

Rather than see all this effort to legitimize study as a distraction from the original purity and simplicity of the Order, Bonaventure saw this as proof of the guidance of the Holy Spirit, reassuring the unknown Master of Theology:

> Let it not disturb you that in the beginning our brothers were simple and unlettered; rather, this very fact ought to strengthen your faith in the Order. For I confess before God that what made me love St Francis's way of life so much

was that it is exactly like the origin and the perfection of the Church itself, which began first with simple fishermen and afterwards developed to include the most illustrious and learned doctors. You find that same thing in the Order of St Francis; in this way God reveals that it did not come about through human calculations but through Christ. For since the works of Christ do not diminish but ceaselessly grow, this undertaking was proved to be God's doing when wise men did not disdain to join the company of simple folk. (Bonaventure, 1994, p. 54)

Steeped in Scripture

So, study, books and libraries became integral parts of what it meant to be Franciscan. Would Francis have approved? Reluctantly perhaps, but nonetheless, I think the answer has to be 'yes'. Francis was steeped in the Scriptures, interpreting almost everything symbolically in accordance with the Bible. Francis once gathered up worms from a path because they reminded him of Jesus who quoted Psalm 22 from the cross, a psalm that begins, 'My God, my God, why have you forsaken me?' and includes the verse: 'I am a worm, and not human.' So also, Francis gathered up fragments of writing in case they contained the Lord's names:

> Wherever I find our Lord's most holy names and written words in unbecoming places, I want to gather them up and I beg that they be gathered up and placed in a becoming place. And we must honour all theologians and those who minister the most holy divine words and respect them as those who minister to us spirit and life. (FA:ED, vol. 1, p. 125)

We saw above how, when he had to make a difficult decision about the path his ministry would take, he would consult the Scriptures, more than once opening the Bible at random to let the Spirit guide him to the appropriate verse. In his preaching, he amazed people by the depth of his knowledge of the Scriptures and was sought after even by more conventionally educated church leaders:

> Another time, when [Francis] was in Rome at the home of a cardinal, he was asked about some obscure passages, and he brought to light their depths in such a way that you would think he was constantly studying the Scriptures. The Lord Cardinal said to him: 'I'm not asking you as a scholar, but as a person who has the Spirit of God, and so I gladly accept the meaning in your answer, because I know it comes from God alone.' (FA:ED, vol. 2, p. 316)

His knowledge of the Scriptures even ferried him over to the other side of death:

> Once when [Francis] was sick and full of pain all over, his companion said to him: 'Father, you have always taken refuge in the Scriptures, and they always have offered you relief from pain. Please, have something from the prophets also read to you now, and maybe your spirit will rejoice in the Lord.' The saint said to him: 'It is good to read the testimonies of Scripture, and it is good to seek the Lord our God in them. But I have already taken in so much of Scripture that I have more than enough for meditating and reflecting. I do not need more, son; I know Christ, poor and crucified.' (FA:ED, vol. 2, p. 316)

Francis loved to ponder the Scriptures, but the book he studied most often was the 'book' of Christ, poor and crucified. He would meditate ceaselessly on the events of the last week of the life of Jesus. And in this we find another clear point of contact between the two saints, Francis and Bonaventure. In the Prologue to his *Breviloquium*, Bonaventure describes the different ways Scripture is read, and how such study enables the Christian to be rooted and grounded in love, that they 'may have the power to comprehend, with all the saints, what is the

breadth and length and height and depth, and to know the love
of Christ that surpasses knowledge, so that you may be filled
with all the fullness of God' (Eph. 3.18–19).

> Holy Scripture – unlike other fields of knowledge – has not
> been circumscribed by the rules of reasoning, defining, and
> dividing; or by being restricted to only part of the universe.
> Rather, it unfolds, by supernatural inspiration, for the sake
> of providing man the wayfarer with as much knowledge
> as he needs to save his soul. Using, therefore, a language
> sometimes literal and sometimes figurative, it sums up, as it
> were, the content of the entire universe. (Bonaventure, 1963,
> pp. 2–3)

For Bonaventure, Scripture is theology, the wisdom that surpasses knowledge, the attentiveness to all things, with love,
that enables all people to be filled with the fullness of God.
And this wisdom is revealed in Christ, the Book of Life (Latin:
liber vitae), in whom 'all things in heaven and on earth were
created ... and through him [Christ] God was pleased to reconcile to himself all things' (Col. 1.16, 20). Indeed, Christ is 'the
power of God and the wisdom of God' (1 Cor. 1.24).

Jesus, the Book of Wisdom

In his devotional meditation manual entitled *The Tree of Life*,
Bonaventure leads his readers through the gospel story of the
life of Jesus, including more general themes for meditation.
From his birth to his resurrection, the life and ministry of Jesus
are lovingly landscaped across a canvas as wide as the human
imagination. Each chapter consists of a reflection on a theme,
interwoven with multicoloured threads of Scripture, and then
closes with a prayer or exhortation to the reader to praise
and worship their redeemer. It is a kind of *lectio divina*, the
monastic practice of reading a text, meditating upon it, letting
it move the reader to prayer and finally entering into the silence

of contemplation. Here is the chapter entitled 'Jesus, Inscribed Book', which is really a hymn to Wisdom, who was present at the foundation of the world (Prov. 8.22–31), playing in the presence of God, delighting in the human race:

> For the glory of the kingdom to be perfect, there is required not only exalted power but also resplendent wisdom so that the government of the kingdom is directed not by arbitrary decision but by the brilliant rays of the eternal laws emanating without deception from the light of wisdom. And this wisdom is written in Christ Jesus as in the book of life, in which God the Father has hidden all the treasures of wisdom and knowledge (Col. 2.3). Therefore, the only-begotten Son of God, as the uncreated Word, is the book of wisdom and the light that is full of living eternal principles in the mind of the supreme Craftsman, as the inspired Word in the angelic intellects and the blessed, as the incarnate Word in rational minds united with the flesh. Thus throughout the entire kingdom the manifold wisdom of God (Eph. 3.10) shines forth from him and in him, as in a mirror containing the beauty of all forms and lights, and as in a book in which all things are written according to the deep secrets of God.
>
> O, if only I could find this book whose origin is eternal, whose essence is incorruptible, whose knowledge is life, whose script is indelible, whose study is desirable, whose teaching is easy, whose knowledge is sweet, whose depth is inscrutable, whose words are ineffable; yet all are a single Word! Truly, whoever finds this book will find life and will draw salvation from the Lord. (Bonaventure, 1978, pp. 169–70)

Bonaventure may have loved books made of parchment and vellum, but the Book he truly loved was the Word of God, crucified and risen. Here he summarizes with intricate precision the doctrine of exemplarism, the teaching that all things shine with the light of Christ, through whom and for whom all things are made (Col. 1.16). Having been brought into being as their true natures emerge from the mind of Christ, all things reflect the creative Wisdom of God. Christ is the template of salvation, the model of God's perfect plan of creation, the 'seed bank' not just of the forests and the fields but of every living thing. It is a Platonic vision of emergence and return, the manifestation of the presence of God and the celebration of the journey home. The teaching of the Greek philosophers Plato and Aristotle was only made available to Bonaventure and his contemporaries because of the rediscovery of the texts by Muslim theologians and their translations of the texts into Arabic. Thus, flowing from Greek into Arabic and then into Latin, a rich stew of theology emerged, flavoured with every spice of Eastern and Western thought. The style is poetic and like all poetry, it is difficult to translate without losing the meaning or the rhetorical flow. Bonaventure writes in Latin, the phrases full of alliteration and assonance, together with scriptural echoes and well-known quotations from earlier theologians such as Augustine, or Dionysius, or Richard of St Victor. Quotations are rarely referenced – that would only hinder the flow – and in any case it was a compliment to one's forebears that their writings were re-used. Modern ideas of plagiarism were not even considered in those days.

In his short treatise *On the Reduction of the Arts to Theology*, Bonaventure explains how theology by right includes all that is good and true in every art and science:

> And so it is evident how the manifold wisdom of God, which is clearly revealed in sacred Scripture, lies hidden in all knowledge and in all nature. It is clear also how all divisions of knowledge are servants of theology, and it is for this reason that theology makes use of illustrations and terms pertaining to every branch of knowledge. It is likewise clear how wide the illuminative way may be, and how the divine reality itself lies hidden within everything which is perceived or known. (Bonaventure, 1996, p. 61)

Theology, for Bonaventure, was not an archaic discourse related to the religions of the world. It is even debateable whether he would have recognized the category of 'religion' as anything other than the faith of Christians. Rather, theology is the essence of all wisdom, wherever knowledge is revealed by the attention of the heart. All the 'arts', which include all that we would now term 'science', all practical knowledge of any kind, if studied with the loving gaze of a disciple of Christ, are 'reduced', that is 'led back' or 'summarized' or 'brought to completion' as theology. Bonaventure spells out this relation of theology to science and wisdom in the first chapter of his *Breviloquium*:

> Theology is the only perfect science, for it begins at the beginning, which is the first Principle [God], and proceeds to the end, which is the final wages paid; ... Theology is also the only perfect wisdom, for it begins with the supreme Cause, considered as the Principle of all things made. This is the point where philosophical knowledge ends, whereas theology goes on to consider this same Cause as the remedy for sin, the reward of merit, and the goal of desire. All Christians should burn with the longing to attain this knowledge, for it is unto souls perfect savour, life, and salvation. (Bonaventure, 1963, p. 34)

Theology is both perfect science and perfect wisdom: it speaks of all aspects of reality, human and divine. Clearly, Bonaventure himself would 'burn with the longing to attain this knowledge'. Theology for him was a passion, not a pastime, a desire that he could taste as he savoured the words of Scripture, an initiation into life in all its fullness (see John 10.10).

'The Soul's Journey into God'

This path of divine wisdom, the study of true theology, is described most fully in Bonaventure's essay 'The Soul's Journey into God (*Itinerarium mentis in Deum*)'. There, in the Prologue, he seeks to draw the reader into the embrace of Christ:

Therefore, I first of all invite the reader to groans of prayer through Christ crucified, through whose blood we are purged from the stain of our sins. Do not think that reading is sufficient without unction, speculation without devotion, investigation without admiration, circumspection without exultation, industry without piety, knowledge without charity, intelligence without humility, study without divine grace, the mirror without the inspiration of divine wisdom. (Bonaventure, 2002, p. 39)

As we have seen above, it is 'knowledge without charity' that Bonaventure is warning against. This is mere information, which has become the focus of so much energy in today's society. Data is the new source of power; but this is 'intelligence without humility'. It is what we do with information that is important. Is it to exert control, to manipulate opinion; or to learn about, appreciate and admire the wonderful diversity of humanity?

Bonaventure sees the universe as a path to follow, a ladder to climb, as well as an inward journey of discovery into the human mind. He summarizes the beginnings of this journey as follows:

It is in harmony with our created condition that the universe itself might serve as a ladder by which we can ascend into God. Among created things, some are vestiges, others are images; some are bodily, others are spiritual; some are temporal, others are everlasting; some are outside us, others are within us. In order to arrive at the First Principle [God] which is most spiritual and eternal, and above us, it is necessary that we move through the vestiges which are bodily and temporal and outside us. And this is to be led in the way of God. Next we must enter into our mind which is the image of God, an image which is everlasting, spiritual and within us. And this is to enter into the truth of God. Finally we must pass beyond to that which is eternal, most spiritual, and above us by raising our eyes to the First Principle. And this will bring us to rejoice in the knowledge of God and to stand in awe before God's majesty. (Bonaventure, 2002, p. 47)

In this passage, Bonaventure outlines some of the basic structures of his book. The six chapters, compared to the six wings of the seraphim seen in a vision by Isaiah (6.2), and seen again by Francis on Mount La Verna, are divided into three pairs, each signifying a different stage of the ascent into God. First to be discovered are the 'vestiges', the footprints of God, seen in the material world. From a footprint in the sand, you can estimate the size and weight of the one who has been there before you, even guess the speed at which they walked or ran; so with the vestiges of God, we can at least know that someone has gone before us, that we are not alone on a deserted beach facing a cold, indifferent ocean. The material world contains shadows, echoes of a reality we dimly perceive, pointers to a precision and order that indicate, to the eyes of faith, one in whom all things hold together.

Then in the next stage of the journey, having discovered how God shines forth in every creature, the attention turns within, to see the signs of God's presence in our minds and hearts:

Therefore, enter into yourself and recognize that your mind loves itself most fervently. But it cannot love itself if it does not know itself. And it would not know itself unless it remembered itself, for we do not grasp anything with our understanding if it is not present to us in our memory. From this you see, not with the eye of the flesh but with the eye of reason, that the soul possesses a threefold power. Now consider the operation of these powers and their relation to each other. Here you can see God through yourself as through an image. And this is to see through a mirror in an obscure manner (cf. 1 Cor. 13.12). (Bonaventure, 2002, p. 81)

Here Bonaventure delineates the three powers of the soul, which echo the powers of God, making the soul an image of the Holy Trinity, as taught by Augustine of Hippo. These three powers are memory, intelligence and will (*memoria, intelligentia et voluntas*), being images of God the Father, Son and Holy Spirit, respectively. From a slightly different perspective, these powers could be described as attention, understanding and love. These powers or faculties enable us to see things as they really are, as explained in the *Breviloquium*: the eye of the flesh seeing the things outside us, the eye of reason seeing within ourselves, and the eye of contemplation seeing what is above us in the divine nature (Bonaventure, 1963, pp. 105–6). It is the eye of reason that enables us to see the image of God in the workings of the human mind.

The power of memory (*memoria*), in particular, is described in an intriguing way by Bonaventure, again following the teaching of his mentor Augustine:

The function of the memory is to retain and represent not only things that are present, corporeal and temporal, but also things that are successive, simple, and eternal. Memory holds past things by recall, present things by reception, future things by means of foresight ... In its first activity, the actual retention of all temporal things, past, present, and future, the memory is similar to eternity, whose undivided presentness extends to all times ... So through the operations of memory, it becomes clear that the soul itself is an image of God and a similitude so present to itself and having God so present to it that it actually grasps God and potentially 'has the capacity for God and the ability to participate in God.' (Bonaventure, 2002, pp. 81–3)

The quote with which Bonaventure finishes this section comes from Augustine's work *De Trinitate*, 'On The Trinity' (XIV, 8:11). Bonaventure reflects on this in his *Commentary on the Sentences* (1 Sent. 3), that the soul is 'capable of God' (*capax Dei*) not because of its substance or essence, but because it is capable of knowledge and love; and both are essential to this participation in God.

At first sight, it would seem that the Franciscan tradition

is all about the discovery of God in creation, about delight in the sun and the moon, the rain and the wind, and all the animals that Francis befriends in his wandering through the woods and fields of Umbria. But here, Bonaventure says that this is only the beginning of the journey. God reveals the divine nature even more unmistakably in the psychological make-up of humanity. In particular, it is in memory, or attention, that God the Father is clearly seen and understood.

The use of the term 'memory' reminds me of the fundamental practice in the search for enlightenment in Buddhism: the practice of 'mindfulness'. This term translates the Sanskrit word *smriti*, which also has the root meaning of 'memory', originally used for the memorization of sacred texts. In its wider sense, memory, in the Indian spiritual traditions, is the practice of continually remembering, calling to mind the object of contemplation, whether it be the transience of the breath, the suffering of attachment, or the insubstantiality of all things in this world. In Christianity, memory, mindfulness, is the image of God, the reflection of the divine being; this is the way to abide in the presence of God in all things. Later Christian tradition coined the word 'recollection' for this kind of prayer: re-collecting the scattered mind and reuniting it with God. And just as we remember God, so God remembers us, gathering us up corporately and individually, making us whole once again.

Then, moving on from the doctrine of the soul's identity as an image of the Trinity, Bonaventure devotes two chapters, the last two 'wings of the Seraphim', to the discovery of God as Being, and as Goodness itself. The scriptural sources for this teaching are first, the apparition of God to Moses at the burning bush (Ex. 3.14), where God reveals himself as YHWH, 'I am who I am', the One Who Is; and second, the teaching of Jesus that 'No one is good but God alone' (Luke 18.19). On the revelation of God as Being Itself, Bonaventure writes:

> Looking over the way we have come, let us say that the most pure and absolute being, because it is being in an unqualified sense, is first and last; and therefore it is the origin and

consummating end of all things. Because it is eternal and most present, it embraces and enters into all things that endure in time, simultaneously existing as their centre and circumference. Because it is most simple and greatest, it is within all things and outside all things, and hence 'it is an intelligible sphere whose centre is everywhere and whose circumference is nowhere.' (Bonaventure, 2002, p. 121)

Here Bonaventure describes a truly lofty vision of the immanence and transcendence of God: that God is both within and above all things, holding all things in being. Again, he is drawing from the wisdom tradition within the Scriptures, particularly from Proverbs 8 and Wisdom 7; but these Judeo-Christian elements also contain many echoes of wisdom traditions from around the world, such as the Taoist *Tao Te Ching*. In this ancient Chinese text, the Way (*Tao*) is said to be: 'the beginning of heaven and earth', and 'the mother of ten thousand things'. 'Ever desireless, one can see the mystery. Ever desiring one can see the manifestations. These two spring from the same source but differ in name; this appears as darkness... the gate to all mystery' (Lao Tsu, 1973, p. 1). The 'ten thousand things' is a reference to the myriad creatures in the universe, revealed by the desire to understand the manifest nature of reality; yet all things have their source in the mysterious Tao, that which holds all things in being, and is known in the equanimity beyond desire.

Bonaventure goes on to describe the understanding of God not just as amorphous being, but as self-diffusive goodness. In this he once more delves into the prayer experience of Francis who cries out to God in *The Praises to Be Said at All the Hours*: 'All-powerful, most holy, most high, supreme God: all good, supreme good, totally good, you who alone are good, may we give you all praise, all glory, all thanks, all honour, all blessing, and all good. So be it! So be it! Amen' (*FA:ED*, vol. 1, p. 162). Because God is goodness, God must radiate out to others and share with them the fullness of life, hence the need for the divine mutuality among the three Persons of the Holy Trinity.

This intuitive sense of God as Being and Good is not a matter of abstract philosophical speculation. Entering into an extended time of retreat in silence, meditation and prayer can often lead to an expanded awareness of the sheer wonder of all things. In the stillness of the mind at unity with itself, the beauty of all things is intimately revealed, like the sparkling of rain drops glistening in the sunshine after a heavy rain. It may be a statement of faith, given the suffering in the world, that Being and Goodness are indissolubly linked, but it is also an affirmation arising out of the experience of contemplative prayer that this is undeniably true.

But even here Bonaventure has not reached the end of his journey. The seventh chapter of his *Itinerarium* seems to take a step backwards, while in fact making a leap forwards into the mystery of redemptive suffering as discovered in Christ and his Passover from death to life:

> All this was shown also to blessed Francis when, in a rapture of contemplation (*in excessu contemplationis*) on the top of the mountain where I reflected on the things I have written here, a six-winged Seraph fastened to a cross appeared to him. This I myself and several others have heard about from the companion who was with him at that very place. Here he was carried out of himself in contemplation and passed over into God. And he has been set forth as the example of perfect contemplation just as he had earlier been known as the example of action, like another Jacob transformed into Israel. So it is that God invites all truly spiritual persons through Francis to this sort of passing over, more by example than by words. (Bonaventure, 2002, p. 135)

The companion who was with Francis when he had the vision of the crucified Seraph and received the stigmata on Mount La Verna was Brother Leo. Of all the friars he was perhaps the one closest to Francis, and the most revered as a living link to the saint. By referring to Leo, Bonaventure is seeking to show the continuity in the Order between Francis and himself, as he meditates on the events that took place there at the mountain hermitage. The experience Bonaventure describes is a passing over like the exodus of the people of Israel out of Egypt, or like Jacob wrestling with the angel at the ford of the Jabbok and being renamed Israel (Gen. 32.22–32). Likewise, it picks up the reference to Jesus at his Transfiguration talking with Moses and Elijah about his approaching exodus at Jerusalem (Luke 9.31). This passing over, or exodus, from death to life is not just the prerogative of the saints like Francis, but is an invitation to all people to share in the saving death and resurrection of Jesus. It is also an entrance into both the darkness of the intellect and the fire of desire:

> If this passing over is to be perfect, all intellectual activities must be given up, and our deepest and total affection must be directed into and transformed into God. But this is mystical and very secret, which no one knows except one who receives it. And no one receives it but one who desires it. And no one desires it but one who is penetrated to the very marrow with the fire of the Holy Spirit whom Christ has sent into the world. (Bonaventure, 2002, p. 137)

This passing over is not just something to be experienced at the resurrection of the righteous to eternal life. It is also the experience of contemplation here and now – the letting go of all intellectual activities, the descent into the divine darkness of the apophatic path, the journey into the unknown yet most intimate God. This final step of the way cannot be accomplished by the self alone, but only by the help of the Holy Spirit, and then only by means of the love poured into our hearts by the Holy Spirit that was given to us (Rom. 5.5). It needs the vision of the crucified to awaken such love and so instead of ending with a neo-Platonic ascent into the unbodied heavens, Bonaventure takes the reader by the hand and leads them back to Jesus crucified, to the one who loved the world even to the end.

Jesus pierced with a lance

Once more, in *The Tree of Life*, Bonaventure returns to the cross of Christ, in a passage drenched with biblical references:

Then, in order that the Church might be formed out of the side of Christ sleeping on the cross and that the words of Scripture might be fulfilled which say: They will look upon him whom they have pierced (John 19.37; Zach. 12.10), the divine plan permitted that one of the soldiers should pierce open his sacred side with a lance. While blood mixed with water flowed, the price of our salvation was poured forth, which gushing from the secret foundation of the heart gave power to the sacraments of the Church to offer the life of grace and to become for those already living in Christ a draught of the fountain of living water springing up into eternal life (John 4.14). Behold how the spear ... made a cleft in the rock and a hollow place in the cliff as an abode for doves (S. of Sol. 2.14).

Rise, therefore, beloved of Christ, be like the dove that makes its nest in the heights in the mouth of a cleft. There, like a sparrow that finds a home, do not cease to keep watch; there, like the turtle dove, hide the offspring of your chaste love; there apply your mouth to draw water from the Saviour's fountains for this is the river arising from the midst of paradise which, divided into four branches and flowing into devout hearts, waters and makes fertile the whole earth. (Bonaventure, 1978, pp. 154–5)

Bonaventure describes Jesus as 'sleeping' on the cross: like a new Adam, from whose side a rib is taken to form Eve his bride, so from Christ crucified the Church is born by the divine plan. And Mary, the new Eve, becomes the representative of Mother Church, in which the believer is fed with the blood and water gushing from the saviour's opened side, the eucharistic mystery of the bread and wine. This cleft, like a hollow in the rock, a dark cave in which to find rest, is the Sacred Heart of

Jesus. From this cave, as from the temple of the Lord, streams of living waters flow, bringing healing to all the nations (see Ezek. 47 and Rev. 22).

This overflowing devotion to the crucified Christ is found again in Bonaventure's open letter to an Abbess, entitled, 'On the Perfection of Life, Addressed to Sisters *(De perfectione vitae ad sorores)*':

Beloved Mother, if devout prayer is to raise your heart even higher and make it burn with still more ardent love for God, consider carefully that three things may lift the soul in ecstasy [*excessus mentis*]: the height of devotion, of admiration, or of exultation. First, the height of devotion sometimes may cause our spirit to lose hold of itself and rise above itself; to pass into a state of rapture [*raptus*] when we are inflamed with the ardour of such celestial desire...

Again, rapture sometimes occurs because of the height of admiration. When our soul is irradiated with divine light, and held in suspense by the wonder of the supreme Beauty, it is thrown off its foundation...

Finally, rapture may come about through the height of exultation. Once our soul has tasted this intimate abundance of internal sweetness, or rather, when it is fully inebriated, it completely forgets what it is and what it was, and its whole being becomes supernatural desire, carried away as it is in a state of wonderful happiness. (Bonaventure, 1960, pp. 237–8)

If nothing else, this passage proves that Bonaventure, for all his studies, has not extinguished 'the spirit of prayer and devotion' which was the sole criterion for Francis to allow the study of theology. In fact, for all its devotional fervour, this is a very literary passage, drawing heavily from the writings of Richard of St Victor (d. 1173). Richard was a canon of the Abbey of St Victor in Paris, and one of the great systematizers of the contemplative path. Richard himself forms one link in a chain of teaching seen among many medieval exegetes and lived out most especially by female mystics such as Margaret of Cortona, whom we met in an earlier chapter.

Here in Bonaventure's letter to his sisters in religion, the two key terms, *excessus mentis* and *raptus*, are closely linked with each other, just as we found in the description of Brother Giles' experience of contemplative prayer. Scriptural antecedents are found in the Latin Vulgate translation of the Bible, in particular in 2 Corinthians 12.2–4, which recounts Paul's being caught up into heaven. This ascent was associated with that of Enoch (Gen. 5.24) and Elijah (2 Kings 2.3, 11), both of whom were miraculously taken up to heaven. Augustine (AD 354–430) twice recounts his own experiences of rapture in his *Confessions*, once on his own and once with his mother Monica, being absorbed in heavenly contemplation. Gregory the Great says in his biography of Benedict of Nursia (480–548) that the founder of Western monasticism experienced both *excessus* and *raptus*. Nearer in time to the Franciscans, the Cistercians also used both terms; Bernard of Clairvaux (1090–1153), in particular, writes of being caught up both in the affective rapture of mercy and compassion, as well as in the noetic rapture, the clear vision of the truth of God more frequently associated with the term rapture in medieval writings.

Yearning for the Light

We mentioned, in the chapter on Margaret of Cortona, the common three-fold classification of the spiritual path into the stages of purgation, illumination and union. Many texts that speak of the foundational stage of the spiritual path, that of purgation, tend to speak of the suffering inherent in desire: how concupiscence, together with malice and negligence, need to be seen clearly as they befog the mind. The remedy for this is self-awareness and confession. But here, writing on the perfection of life in the illuminative and unitive way, Bonaventure speaks of the value of supernatural desire, a theme taken up more fully in his *Collations on the Six Days* (*Collationes in Hexaemeron*):

> The door to wisdom is a yearning (*concupiscentia*) and vehement desire (*desiderium*) for it. Hence in the Psalm: Open your mouth, and I will fill it. This is the way by which wisdom comes into me, by which I go into wisdom, and wisdom enters into me, just like charity (*caritas*). Hence God is charity, and those who abide in charity abide in God, and God in them. But, this wisdom cannot be possessed without the highest pleasure; and where there is the highest pleasure, the highest yearning precedes it. (Bonaventure, 2018, p. 120)

For Bonaventure, yearning and desire are qualities necessary to journey fully into God. This is not a dry, intellectual pursuit. Desire and pleasure are at root good, however misdirected they may be in daily life. This is why the biblical book Song of Songs is so often commented on by writers on contemplation. Bernard of Clairvaux is a classic example of this. Ultimately, for the Cistercians and Franciscans, it is the experience of love that is the final refuge, not understanding. Bonaventure continues in his *Collationes in Hexaemeron*:

> And there is a most secret operation transcending all understanding (*intellectum*); because nobody knows (*scit*) it unless it is experienced. For in the soul (*anima*) there are several apprehending powers: the sensitive, the imaginative, the estimative, the intellective; and all must be relinquished, and at the summit is the union of love (*unitio amoris*), and this transcends all. Hence is it clear that total beatitude is not in the intellective [power]... This love (*amor*) transcends all understanding (*intellectum*) and knowledge (*scientiam*). (Bonaventure, 2018, p. 131)

From the outside, the experience of rapture can seem like a kind of stupor, an absence of consciousness, a sleep that is oblivious to whatever is happening. But from the inside, for the one experiencing the rapture, there is an awful lot going on. The outward senses may be stilled, but the spiritual senses are working overtime. The mind may be as if asleep, but the heart is wide awake:

> When the mind (*mens*) is joined to God in that union, in some way it sleeps, and in some way it remains awake: *I sleep, but my heart is awake* [S. of Sol. 5.2]. Only the affective [power] (*affectiva*) is awake and imposes silence upon all the other powers; then a person is alienated from the senses and is placed in ecstasy (*ecstasi*), and hears secret words that no person may say [2 Cor. 12.4] because they are only in the affect (*affectu*). Hence, since nothing can be expressed unless it is conceived, nor conceived unless it is understood, and [here] understanding (*intellectus*) is silent; it follows that one can say and explain practically nothing. (Bonaventure, 2018, p. 131)

The quality of ineffability is almost universally applied to such experiences. As the *Tao Te Ching* famously says, 'The one who speaks does not know; the one who knows does not speak' (see Lao Tsu, 1973, p. 56). This is the apophatic way, the way of negation, saying that God is 'not this, not that' (Sanskrit: *neti neti*). And yet negation is not the end of the journey, at least not for Franciscans. Ultimately for Bonaventure, as for Francis before him, there is the wordless affirmation of love:

> Love (*amor*) always comes after negation ... one who sculpts a figure adds nothing; rather, he removes and leaves in the stone itself a noble and beautiful form. Thus, does the knowledge (*notitia*) of divinity, through negation, leave in us the most noble disposition ... This then is the form of wisdom; these are the mental excesses (*excessus*). (Bonaventure, 2018, p. 134)

Rapture chips away all that is not eternal, all that is not love. The overflowing of love leads us, ultimately, through the darkness into the inextinguishable radiance of God's light.

To close this chapter, we return with Bonaventure to the *Tree of Life* and the source of everlasting light:

> In this eternal kingdom, all good and perfect gifts come down in plenty and abundance from the Father of Lights (James 1.17) through Jesus Christ ... For he is a pure effusion of the brightness of the power of the omnipotent God, and therefore nothing that is sullied can enter (Wisd. 7.25) into this Fountain-Ray of light.
>
> You soul devoted to God, whoever you are, run with living desire to this Fountain of life and light and with the innermost power of your heart cry out to him: 'O inaccessible beauty of the most high God and the pure brightness of the eternal light, life vivifying all life, light illumining every light, and keeping in perpetual splendour a thousand times a thousand lights brilliantly shining before the throne of your Divinity since the primeval dawn! O eternal and inaccessible, clear and sweet stream from the fountain hidden from the eyes of all mortals, whose depth is without bottom, whose height is without limit, whose breadth cannot be bounded, whose purity cannot be disturbed.' From this Fountain flows the stream of the oil of gladness, which gladdens the city of God, and the powerful fiery torrent, the torrent, I say, of the pleasure of God, from which the guests at the heavenly banquet drink to joyful inebriation and sing without ceasing hymns of jubilation.
>
> Anoint us with the sacred oil, and refresh with the longed-for waters of this torrent the thirsting throat of our parched hearts, so that amid shouts of joy and thanksgiving we may sing to you a canticle of praise, proving by experience that with you is the fountain of life, and in your light we will see light. (Bonaventure, 1978, pp. 170–2)

6

The Visionary: Angela of Foligno (1248–1309)

The thirteenth century was a time for a new monasticism. Groups such as the Beguines, and the Third Order Regular of the Franciscans and Dominicans, were finding new ways of creating community. They were united by a rule of common prayer and service, but without necessarily taking life vows or vows of stability, and with various degrees of enclosure and poverty. Situated just outside the more strictly controlled environments of established monastic communities, they experienced a freedom in their intense explorations of prayer and identification with the poor as they sought to follow Christ. Often they spoke of the need for reconciliation and peace: the Franciscan Tertiaries, for example, being forbidden to carry arms.

This new monasticism articulated a more widely felt credibility gap between the institutional Church and the religious experience and aspirations of the laity. The poverty movement itself, of which Francis was a part, was both a protest against the affluence of the church hierarchy and an attempt to live out the poverty of Jesus, his mother and his disciples, which they saw depicted in the Gospels. No longer were people content to simply follow the descriptions in the Acts of the Apostles of new converts laying all their wealth at the feet of Peter and forming a stable, controlled community of prayer. They wanted to be poor and homeless like the wandering Christ and his disciples, sharing in his mission to preach the gospel of the Kingdom of God, and united to him particularly in the ultimate poverty of the cross.

Furthermore, the thirteenth century was a time of a new 'women's movement'. With the crusades, and continuing grinding wars in Europe, many women were left at home to run the family estates. Their power and influence inevitably increased during this time. Women also joined religious communities in much greater numbers, particularly the Beguines, semi-independent communities of women gathered around a Mistress as their leader. Their spirituality was deeply rooted in the everyday realities of life: in the humanity of Christ and particularly his physical suffering, and in the practice of fasting and feasting, often linked to eucharistic devotion. Solitaries too were flourishing, as evidenced by the publication of the *Ancrene Wisse*, a Rule for anchorites (solitary hermits) such as the later Julian of Norwich (1343–c. 1416).

This is the background to the life of the extraordinary Franciscan mystic, Angela of Foligno. Angela held a pivotal place in the transmission of the Franciscan charism. She was of the second generation of Franciscans, part of the process of creating a viable form to enable the spirit of St Francis to live on. She was born in 1248 of a wealthy family and was, by her own later admission, rich, proud and vain. In 1285, at the age of 37, she was converted to a life of penance, eventually taking the habit of the Third Order of the Franciscans in 1291. During the years 1290 to 1296 she met with her cousin, the Observant friar Arnaldo, mostly in the Church of St Francis at Foligno, to tell of her experiences and visions in prayer. These were somewhat surreptitious meetings, Arnaldo feeling the suspicions of his fellow friars as he hastily scribbled down her Umbrian dialect reminiscences in the Latin of the Church. Angela described a journey of 30 steps, which Arnaldo revised in what is now called *The Memorial*, to make 19 steps up to their first collaboration plus seven supplementary steps, eventually leading to full union with God. The journey was not an easy one for Angela. She confesses to Arnaldo:

You need to be aware also that each of these steps takes time. It is indeed very pitiful and truly heart-breaking that the soul is so sluggish and moves so painfully and ponderously toward God. It takes such tiny steps at a time. As for myself, I lingered and wept at each step. My only consolation was being able to weep, but it was a bitter consolation. (Angela, 1993, p. 125)

One of the reasons Angela's writings are so accessible is her honesty and fallibility. She does not find the spiritual life easy. It is a struggle from one end to the other and she never hesitates to admit her faults and perplexity at every stage of the way. The work was a collaboration from the start and that also gives it much of its charm, with Arnaldo frequently adding asides that he could only barely understand or give words to the wonderful things that Angela was telling him. But he also guided her, asking her to clarify her meaning and challenging her to reflect more on what she had experienced.

Added to the description of Angela's experiences in 'The Memorial' are a series of 'Instructions', often in the form of letters addressed to the friars who came to her for direction. One of these was Ubertino da Casale, a prominent figure among the Spirituals, who said of Angela:

She restored, even a thousand-fold, all the gifts of my soul that I had lost through my sinfulness, so that from henceforth I was not the same man as before. When I had experienced the splendour of her ardent virtue, she changed the whole face of my mind; and so drove out weakness and languor from my soul and body, and renewed my mind that was torn asunder with distractions, that no one who had known me before could doubt that the spirit of Christ was begotten anew within me through her. (Quoted in Underhill, 1925, p. 100)

In *The Memorial* and *Instructions*, making together the *Book of the Blessed Angela of Foligno*, Angela and Arnaldo between them have created a masterpiece of mystical literature, ranking among the most important texts of the High Middle Ages.

Evelyn Underhill, the Anglican pioneer of studies of mysticism, said of her:

> Angela of Foligno [is] in many respects the most remarkable of the great Franciscan mystics. The redeeming character of Franciscan enthusiasm – its ability to change, brace, and expand the most unlikely spirits and impel them to exacting discipline and selfless work – are fully shown in her. (Underhill, 1925, pp. 99–100)

Underhill believed that Angela's best writing was the equal of anything by Ruysbroek (her great hero among mystics) and far beyond the writings of Teresa of Avila. More recently, Bernard McGinn, in his series on the history of Western Christian mysticism, speaks of Angela's *Book* as 'the premier text of all Franciscan women mystics' and her description of union with God as 'one of the richest ... in Christian history' (McGinn, 1998, pp. 141, 145).

At the foot of the cross

In order to begin to know Angela better for ourselves, we can do no better than look to the startling revelations of the ninth step, where she resolves to stand at the foot of the cross, as a sinner finding refuge. She realized that this would entail letting go of all attachments, whether to people, possessions, even to her very self, so that she would be free to give her heart to Christ. In the end, the process of letting go was more rapid than she had expected. She put away her best clothes and fine food, but there was more to relinquish:

> By the will of God at that time my mother died; she was a great hindrance to me in following the way of God. My husband died also and shortly afterwards all my children. Because I had set out to follow the way I have spoken of, I prayed that God might free me of them, and I was consoled

when they died, although I was very grieved at their deaths. But because God had shown me his grace I imagined that now my heart and my will were united to his heart and his will. (Gallyon, 2000, p. 19)

Angela begins, like Francis, at the foot of the cross. There she finds a refuge amid her consciousness of sin. But then she comes up against the opposition of her family. In those days, marriage was not necessarily a union of love. The average age at marriage at that time was 15 years for women but 30 for men, and the contract would often have been arranged by others. And the fact of her family's sudden death is perhaps not so surprising in an age of sickness and rudimentary medical care. Having experienced the chaos that the Covid-19 pandemic brought to the world, we can better imagine the effect of endless waves of lethal illnesses sweeping across continents with none of the benefits of modern medicine. Nonetheless, at a later step, Angela does say that it was harder to lose her family than she admitted at the time. At the First Supplementary Step she says: 'The thought of continuing to live was a greater burden for me to bear than the pain and sorrow I had felt over the death of my mother and my sons, and beyond any pain that I could imagine' (Angela, 1993, p. 143). Losing her entire family would have been a catastrophic loss for Angela, but perhaps one that she was able to come to terms with through her dialogues with Christ on the cross.

As Angela progresses in her journey, she steels herself to really get serious about her spiritual life, as recounted in her twelfth step:

In order to come to the cross, as I had been inspired to do, I resolved to relinquish everything. This resolve was put into my mind in a most marvellous way by God, for I now began to cherish a strong desire to become poor. My zeal for poverty became so great that I was afraid I might die before I had attained this state, and yet I was assailed by temptations against such a state. A voice whispered to me in my mind saying that I was young and that begging for money might lead me into great danger and bring shame upon me, and that I might be compelled to die of hunger, cold and nakedness. Furthermore all my friends tried to dissuade me from doing such a thing. (Gallyon, 2000, p. 20)

Nonetheless, Angela resolves that come what may, even if she has to die of hunger, or be covered with shame, as long as God was calling her to this path, she would follow it to her dying breath. How many times are such resolutions made! But so often we are too sensible and nothing comes of our resolve. Francis faced similar temptations at the beginning of his conversion. *The Legend of the Three Companions* relates:

There was in Assisi a deformed, hunchbacked woman, whom the devil, appearing to the man of God, recalled to him. He threatened to inflict him with her deformity unless he reneged on the plan he had conceived. But the very brave knight of Christ, shunning the devil's threats, prayed all the more fervently within the cave that God would direct his path. (*FA:ED*, vol. 2, p. 75)

Giles of Assisi also had times of great fear, if not terror, in his wrestling with the forces of evil in his prayers, as we saw in an earlier chapter. Likewise, Clare was tempted to give up her commitment to prayer. The following story echoes the responses of Jesus when tempted in the wilderness, but with a twist of humour that deflates the self-importance of the devil:

After Matins, while Clare was praying, bathed as usual in a stream of tears, the deceitful admonisher approached. 'You should not cry so much,' he said, 'otherwise your brain will dissolve and flow through your nose, because you will have a crooked nose.' To which she responded quickly, 'Whoever knows the Lord suffers nothing that is twisted.' Immediately he fled and vanished. (*CA:ED*, p. 273)

These dialogues are typical of the sayings and stories of the desert fathers and mothers of Egypt, Palestine and Syria in the early centuries of the Church. The power of evil is taken seriously, but not allowed to take control of the lives of the saints. Evagrius, one of the great teachers of the ascetic life, wrote an entire book of useful retorts to confound the devil in any situation of temptation, the title being *Antirrhetikos* or *How To Talk Back*.

Inebriated by the blood of Christ

Angela then goes on to demonstrate the intimate link between devotion to the crucified Christ and meeting with Christ in the Eucharist:

> As I persevered in my prayers I was granted a dream as I slept and in that dream the heart of Christ was revealed to me and I was told that there was no falsehood in that heart, but only truth. He showed me too the wound in his side and he said to me, 'Put your mouth to the wound in my side.' Then it seemed to me that I did put it there and I drank the blood that flowed freshly from his side, and as I did so it was impressed upon me that by this blood I was made clean. (Gallyon, 2000, pp. 20–1)

Again, we are with Christ on the cross and the life of Christ is imbibed with the blood that flows from his side. We have already seen similar sentiments in the chapter on Bonaventure. In medieval art there are depictions of blood flowing from the open wound of Christ into a chalice held by a saint, usually a woman. This was all part of the legend of the Holy Grail, referring to the cup used at the Last Supper and then again to collect the sacred blood from Christ on the cross. Angela dispenses even with the medium of the cup and drinks directly from Christ's wounded side.

Engaging in devotion to Christ in the Blessed Sacrament was a distinctly Franciscan practice, seen in nearly every chapter of this book. It is possible that Francis attended the Fourth Lateran Council of 1215 in Rome, where the doctrine of transubstantiation (the transformation of the eucharistic bread and wine into the body and blood of Christ) was defined. The Council also decreed that churches and church vessels should be kept clean – Francis was known to carry a broom when he went on mission to a church – and the reserved sacrament should be kept safe, also a concern of Francis, who encouraged his friars to take a pyx on their journeys, that is, a box to contain the blessed wafers, in case of need.

Give us this day our daily bread

Later, Angela talks more of the mechanics of her prayer, describing how the simple phrases of the Lord's Prayer could transport her to the heights of contemplation, reciting the words slowly and consciously (see Angela, 1993, p. 129), just as we have seen with Margaret of Cortona. A little further on, Angela reveals more of her spiritual practice:

> At the last stage of my enlightenment I began to comprehend God more vividly and to experience visions and to hear him speaking to me. I took such delight in prayer that sometimes I forgot to eat. I wished that there need be no necessity to eat, so that I might always be at prayer, and indeed I was sometimes tempted not to eat, or to eat very little, but then I perceived that this was a snare which I must avoid. Yet there was such a fire of love in my heart that I never grew tired of being on my knees, or performing some penance or other. (Gallyon, 2000, pp. 22–3)

Here Angela exemplifies the traditional penitential practices of fasting, vigils and constant prayer. But notice that she is much more moderate than many mystics of her day. Where others, like Saint Clare, would fast to the detriment of their health (Francis directed her to eat at least a morsel of bread each day), Angela sees extreme fasting as a temptation. Indeed, the monument on her tomb depicts her as rather plump – at least, nowhere near anorexic. The contemporary stories of women such as Lidwina of Schiedam (1380–1433), and even the much more recent Therese Neumann (d. 1962), fasting for years on end, sustained only by the bread of the Eucharist, are far from Angela's experience.

It is the Passion of Christ that continues to move her most:

> It often happened that when God was spoken of I uttered great cries, even if I was in the company of others, no matter who they were. When people said I was out of my mind I replied that I was sick and could not help myself, for I was ashamed of the way I cried out like this. Also when I saw a picture of the Passion of Christ, I could scarcely control myself and was seized with a kind of fever and fell sick. Because of this my companion hid paintings of the Passion so that I might not see them. During these periods of crying, however, I was granted many visions, consolations and insights. (Gallyon, 2000, p. 23)

Although there are questions that could be asked about Angela's mental health – evidenced in her falling ill or crying out loudly on seeing a religious picture – these vignettes do reveal a person who takes her Christianity with extreme seriousness. Angela couldn't have walked through a gallery with a guide book in her hand, vaguely interested in the history of art. Depictions of the Passion of Christ are for her direct portals into the beating heart of Jesus. And through all the highs and lows of her spiritual and emotional life, Angela remains self-aware and growing in self-knowledge. She questions herself and allows others to question her, without knowing the answers. And there is a quiet, self-deprecating humour underlying it all – just imagine her poor, much put-upon companion, chasing round the house turning over all the religious pictures, trying in vain to keep a lid on Angela's irrepressible devotion to Christ.

Pilgrim to Assisi

After the first 19 steps along Angela's journey, the reader of her *Book* comes to an account of a revelation from the Holy Spirit and a fateful experience in the Church of St Francis in Assisi. She relates the events of a pilgrimage to Assisi, asking that she might feel Christ's presence more clearly, later classified by Arnaldo as part of her First Supplementary Step. When she gets to the crossroads between Spello and Assisi, she hears the Holy Spirit saying to her that he will accompany her every step of the path to Assisi and will speak to her many things. Then, after a few more encouragements to proceed, the Spirit begins to confide in her more intimately:

> 'My daughter, you are sweet to me, you are my temple, my delight. Love me, my beloved daughter! For I greatly love you, and more than you love me.' Very often he said to me: 'My daughter, my sweet spouse, I love you better than any other in the valley of Spoleto, and because I have rested and reposed in you, do you also rest and repose in me!' (Gallyon, 2000, p. 26)

These words of the Holy Spirit are full of warmth and affection. God speaks to Angela as bridegroom to bride. Such bridal mysticism was quite common in her day. Contemporary female writers, such as Hadewijch (thirteenth century) or Mechtild of Magdeburg (c. 1207–c. 1282/1294), frequently used the poetry of courtly love to describe their relationship with God. Apart from this instance, however, Angela is sparing in her use of such language. Perhaps her experience of marriage was too prosaic to be translated into heavenly poems of Love. But the touching homeliness of her relationship with God is affecting in its innocence. The Holy Spirit loves her more than any other woman in the valley of Spoleto. She is at once the Virgin Mary being greeted by the Archangel Gabriel and a humble shepherd's sweetheart having sweet nothings whispered in her ear by the Holy Spirit of God.

This sense of euphoria carries Angela into the Basilica of Saint Francis in Assisi where she has a further vision of the majesty of God; but then the vision begins to fade and she is left desolate.

> Then he departed from me, not suddenly, but slowly and gradually and with great gentleness. But when he had gone I fell down and began to cry out with a loud voice, clamouring and calling out unashamedly, 'Why, oh Love, do you leave me in this manner? Before now I have never known you.' More than this I could not speak, for my voice was suffocated with crying and I could hardly utter these words. (Gallyon, 2000, p. 28)

At this point, Arnaldo, then living at the Sacro Convento, the main conventual Franciscan friary in Assisi, comes rushing out to see what all the commotion is about. To his great consternation he sees that it is his cousin making all this noise; and when she comes back to her senses he sends her away, telling her in his shame never to visit Assisi again. But later he thinks again of his sternness and seeks her out to listen to her story in her own words. And so begins the friendship which flowers in the production of Angela's *Book*.

This whole narrative of Angela's pilgrimage to Assisi is reminiscent of Sermon 74 on the Song of Songs by Bernard of Clairvaux, where the Cistercian saint speaks of the times when he feels the Word of God, 'the Bridegroom', visit his soul:

> I tell you that the Word has come even to me – I speak in my foolishness – and that he has come more than once. Yet however often he has come, I have never been aware of the moment of his coming. I have known he was there; I have remembered his presence afterward; sometimes I had an inkling that he was coming. But I never felt it, nor his leaving

me. And where he comes from when he enters my soul, or where he goes when he leaves it, and how he enters and leaves, I frankly do not know. (Bernard, 1987, pp. 254–5)

This is an altogether more peaceful experience than that of Angela. Bernard says a little later in this sermon that he is made aware of the Word's presence by the sensation of a mysterious warmth deep within him. Then, as the Bridegroom departs, the warmth fades, leaving him weak and cold within. All this he records in a sermon for which the text is the single word 'Return', from the second chapter of the Song of Songs, and it has taken him 73 sermons to reach this far!

Pregnant with God

From this stage on, the visionary aspects of her faith become more evident in the life of Angela. In the Second Supplementary Step, when she is about to recite the Our Father, she hears a voice saying to her, 'You are full of God', and she sees that the whole world is indeed full of God's presence, which fills her with great joy. Brother Arnaldo wants to know more, and tries to get Angela to explain the vision in more detail, and she shares as much as she can:

> I saw a fullness, a brightness with which I felt myself so filled that words fail me, nor can I find anything to compare it with. I cannot tell you that I saw something with a bodily form, but he was as he is in heaven, namely of such an indescribable beauty that I do not know how to describe it to you except as the Beauty and the All Good. (Angela, 1993, pp. 151–2)

This experience of being flooded with a supernatural light is a common theme in mystical literature. It goes back at least as far as the vision recorded in the first chapter of the book of Ezekiel, where the prophet sees the *Shekinah*, the luminous presence of God, as 'something like gleaming amber, something that looked like fire, the appearance of the likeness of the glory of the Lord'. It is this glory that shines all around as the angel announces the birth of Jesus in the Gospel of Luke (2.9) and that surrounds Paul as he falls to the ground on the Damascus road (Acts 9.3–5). It is the uncreated light of the Transfiguration which Jesus is surely describing when he says: 'Your eye is the lamp of your body. If your eye is healthy, your whole body is full of light ... If then your whole body is full of light, with no part of it in darkness, it will be as full of light as when a lamp gives you light with its rays' (Luke 11.34, 36). Jesus seems to speak here of an experience that was not unique to himself, but accessible even to his followers. Angela sees the whole world as flooded by the incandescent brightness of the presence of God. As ever, she expresses herself with the physicality of her body:

> When I was plunged into that previous darkness, I lay flat on the ground, but when I was in the state of greatest illumination, I stood straight up on my feet, on the very tips of my big toes. I was so joy-filled, and my body felt so agile, healthy, invigorated, that I had never experienced anything like it. (Angela, 1993, p. 177)

Full of the divine light, Angela feels she is enabled to see the destiny of all creatures, to understand something of the workings of God's power and goodness. Later, this light manifests itself physically, as recounted by Angela's companion: '[Her] appearance became white, radiant, joyful and flushed, and her eyes became large and were so radiant that she did not seem at all to be herself' (Mazzoni, 1999, p. 63). The whole experience is rather overwhelming for her companion, who is terrified that someone will come and see Angela like this. She suggests that Angela hide herself, as her eyes were like candles. But Angela calmly reassures her companion, saying gently that God will help them if anyone should see them.

At the Fourth Supplementary Step, Angela describes one of the greatest visions of her *Book*:

[God's divine voice] later added, 'I want to show you something of my power.' And immediately the eyes of my soul were opened, and I saw the single fullness of God in which I comprehended the whole world (that is, the land on both sides of the sea, the depths of the sea, the sea itself, everything). And in the entire world I discerned nothing but divine power – the experience is completely indescribable. Then my soul in a state of awe cried out, 'This world is pregnant with God!' And I comprehended the whole world (that is, the land on both sides of the sea, the depths of the sea, the sea itself, everything) as something small, but that the power of God fills and surpasses everything. (Mazzoni, 1999, pp. 54–5)

Then, having shown Angela his power, God goes on to show her his humility in making himself present in the sacrament of the Eucharist and she is struck with remorse at her own pride. She feels herself to be totally unworthy to receive communion, and yet she hears God saying to her at the elevation of the host, the lifting up of the sacred body of Christ at the altar:

And when it was nearly time for the elevation of the Body of Christ, he said, 'See, my divine power is now present above the altar. Indeed I am within you; and although you are receiving me, you have already received me. Receive communion with the blessing of the Father, Son, and Holy Spirit. I who am worthy make you worthy.' And then an indescribable sweetness and intense joy settled within me, and I believe they will remain within me my entire life. (Mazzoni, 1999, p. 55)

Evelyn Underhill described this as, 'a passage unique in the literature of mysticism – the twofold revelation of an Absolute at once humble and omnipotent, personal and transcendent – the unimaginable synthesis of unspeakable power and deep humility' (Underhill, 1911, p. 252). But I don't think it is quite without parallel. It reminds me of Julian of Norwich and her image of the whole universe as a hazelnut held in the palm of God, so fragile and yet enduring simply because God loves it and will continue to love it for ever.

This particular vision of Angela takes place at a celebration of the Eucharist, as so many visions of Angela and her contemporaries did. Francis himself was deeply moved by the humility of God in the Eucharist. In his *Letter to the Entire Order*, he writes:

> O sublime humility! O humble sublimity! The Lord of the universe, God and the Son of God, so humbles himself that for our salvation he hides himself under an ordinary piece of bread! Brothers, look at the humility of God, and pour out your hearts before him! (*FA:ED*, vol. 1, p. 118)

Angela too is deeply moved by the humility of God. There is something about that exclamation of hers: 'This world is pregnant with God!' that startles with its freshness. It comes directly from her experience in life and it is a voice that resonates even today. It is a welcome challenge to much medieval writing of the 'higher' calling of virginity. Angela says that she feels unworthy to receive such revelations of God's presence in all things, that she is 'nothing at all'. And yet it is not God's power that evokes her sense of nothingness so much as God's humility that inspires such awe within her. God chooses to be found in the womb of creation as in the womb of a woman, and in the grain of a loaf of bread made holy by the Author of Life. Angela is made worthy by God and in a sense, she communes with God even before she receives communion. God is already within her by his humility and his power; God chooses to indwell her and all things, and delights to do so. To use a phrase of Augustine of Hippo, she receives what she already is, the body of Christ (Sermon 272).

Gazing at the Crucified

Later in this Fourth Step, Angela speaks of another lodestone of her faith: the cross. Again, it occurs in a liturgical setting during the Office of Vespers, the early evening prayers:

I was gazing at Christ on the cross and looking at him with my bodily eyes, when suddenly my soul was kindled with such a fervent love that even the limbs of my body were affected. I saw and felt that Christ was embracing my soul with his arm, even the arm with which he was crucified. This caused me to rejoice with tremendous joy, greater than any I had hitherto known. (Gallyon, 2000, p. 42)

Like her mentor Francis, Angela returns again and again to Christ on the cross. She vividly sees his body: here it is his hand, in a previous vision it had been his neck: 'The beauty of that throat [of Christ on the cross] was something most wonderful and ineffable' (Gallyon, 2000, p. 34). She sees these things with startling clarity and feels the joy of Christ's presence in her whole body. In this respect she is like the English hermit Richard Rolle (c. 1300–1349), who is full of the warmth, sweetness and song of Christ's presence. At the beginning of his book *The Fire of Love*, he relates how this warmth first startled him and he put his hand to his chest to see if he was really burning up (Rolle, 1972, p. 45). The joy that Angela feels also echoes that of Julian and the warmth of Jesus' declaration to her that he suffered all this for love, and that if he could have suffered more, he would have. Angela continues:

Even now when I am rapt in this vision and the thought of that embrace, my soul is so filled with joy that I can feel no sadness at all at the remembrance of Christ's Passion, though I see the wounds in his hands. All my joy rests in Christ crucified, and sometimes it seems to my soul that in the close embrace that I have spoken of, my soul enters into the side of Christ. (Gallyon, 2000, p. 42)

Angela seems to creep into the wound in Christ's side, as if into a cave, finding there a refuge and peace. This idea is also expressed in the prayer *Anima Christi*, possibly written by Pope John XXII in the early fourteenth century, in the phrase 'Soul of Christ, sanctify me; Body of Christ, save me ... Within your wounds, hide me.' Devotion to the five wounds of Christ was very prevalent in the thirteenth century and is something we find in the writings of Bonaventure, among others. It endures today particularly in devotion to the Sacred Heart, a common Catholic practice popularized in its modern form by Margaret Mary Alacoque in the eighteenth century, but with origins going back to Bernard of Clairvaux and others in the twelfth century. Here we have another instance of the influence of Cistercian spirituality on the early Franciscans.

Like Bonaventure, Angela is devoted to the wounds of Christ, finding there a place of refuge and delight. It is a very visceral experience for her, a physical faith, not an intellectual abstraction. She is embraced by the wounded body of Jesus; she even enters into that body, as Christ's body enters into hers in the Eucharist. All her sadness is turned to joy, not just in participating in Christ's resurrection, but by sharing in his sufferings and his overflowing love for the world.

Such experiences of bliss are deepened yet further in Angela's Fifth Supplementary Step, where she talks of a love about which, paradoxically, she says she can say nothing. Nonetheless she has to say something, even if the words are inadequate to express the joy she feels, as she tries to communicate this abiding in love:

> When that love leaves me I nonetheless remain so totally contented, so angelic, that I can love reptiles, toads, serpents, and even devils. Whatever I see happening, even mortal sin, does not disturb me; that is, it causes me no displeasure, for I believe that God in his justice permits it. And even if a dog were to devour me, I would not care, and it seems to me that I would not feel the pain or suffer from it. This state is higher than standing at the foot of the cross as blessed Francis did. (Angela, 1993, p. 184)

Experiences like these were a source of great joy and love to Angela. The Passion has not led to a bitterness of spirit or a hatred for those who caused such pain. Rather there is only the overwhelming awareness of God's love. It is a universal experience that true contemplative prayer has an innate momentum out into the world in love and compassion. Kindness is the hallmark of the person of prayer. Back in the early centuries of the Church, many great writers on the spiritual life witnessed to this. Isaac of Syria (seventh century), a hermit from the deserts of what is now northern Iraq, wrote movingly in words very similar to those of Angela:

> A merciful heart is the heart's burning for the sake of the entire creation, for people, for birds, for animals, for demons, and for every created thing; and at the recollection and sight of them, the eyes of the merciful pour forth abundant tears. From the strong and vehement mercy that grips their heart and from their great compassion, their heart is humbled and they cannot bear to hear or to see any injury or slight sorrow in creation. For this reason they offer up prayers with tears continually even for irrational beasts, for the enemies of the truth, and for those who harm them, that they be protected and receive mercy. And in like manner they even pray for the reptiles, because of the great compassion that burns without measure in their heart in the likeness of God. (Isaac, 2011, p. 491)

Like Isaac, Angela knows something of this immense compassion of God that floods the whole of creation, a message that needs rediscovering today more than ever. She is also bold enough to say that this state is higher than that of Francis standing at the foot of the cross. To be a true Franciscan is to see the direction in which the teachings of Francis point, beyond the cross, beyond enmity, to the all-embracing compassion of God.

Angela speaks of this compassion again in a further revelation:

> Another way in which the soul knows that God is within it is by an embrace which God gives the soul. Never has

a mother embraced her child with such love, nor can any person from this world be imagined who could give such a loving embrace. God embraces the soul with a love that is unspeakably greater; he presses the soul to himself so sweetly and so lovingly that I don't believe that anyone in the world could believe it, unless they had this experience. (Mazzoni, 1999, p. 62)

Once more we hear echoes of the later Julian ('As truly as God is our father, so truly is God our mother') and of the motherhood of God celebrated in Isaiah 66.13 ('As a mother comforts her child, so I will comfort you'). Angela, a mother of four sons, knew something of what this meant. Francis, too, spoke of his brothers as being like mothers and sons, in his *Rule for Hermitages*. Perhaps Francis had taken the idea from the Cistercians, who described the ideal abbot as a mother to his monks; or maybe for Francis it was just the fruit of the closeness of his relationship with his own mother Pica, or his prayers to the Blessed Virgin Mary, the mother of God.

Into the dark

Up to this point, Angela's *Book* has seemed a general progression onwards and upwards, further into experiences of joy and love: not quite all sweetness and light, but certainly deepening by degrees her sense of the presence of God. At this point, however, she descends into a time of bleak darkness as described in the Sixth Supplementary Step:

I perceive that demons hold my soul in a state of suspension; just as a hanged man has nothing to support him, so my soul does not seem to have any supports left. The virtues of my soul are undermined, while my soul sees it and knows it and watches it happening. And when it perceives all its virtues being subverted and departing, and it can do nothing to prevent this process, the pain and the anger that it feels pushes it to such a point of despair that at times it cannot weep and at other times it weeps inconsolably ... It wails and cries out to God repeatedly and unceasingly: 'My son, my son, do not abandon me, my son!' (Angela, 1993, pp. 197–8)

When she is in this darkness, Angela even cries out for death, even if it means being sent to hell. Already it feels to her as though God has abandoned her, and she just wants God to put an end to her misery. This may be related to the experience of what St John of the Cross calls 'the dark night of the soul'. Liturgically, it is enacted every Good Friday, entering the abandonment of Christ on the cross through the words of the psalms, such as Psalm 88.18: 'You have caused friend and neighbour to shun me; my companions are in darkness.' It is a feeling of complete helplessness: the soul watches its dissolution and is powerless to act. It is filled with anger, despair and rage, as well as fear and grief for the sense of having lost all connection with God. All the raw emotions, the shadow of a pious religious personality, gush out from within. Angela cries out, 'My son, my son, do not abandon me, my son!' echoing both the cry of Jesus from the cross and the agony of grief felt by King David mourning the death of his son Absalom (2 Sam. 18.33). Again, it is through her own life experience that she relates to God, the memory of her own loss in young adulthood making a prism through which to see and experience the God who has also now left her desolate. She even cries out for hell, as if it might give her some relief. Worst of all, she sees no purpose in all of this, no reason for God to allow this to happen.

Then she even loses her sense of self-worth as all her previous virtues are considered by her as nothing but pride and conceit. She is consumed with bitterness and doubt and believes that there is no real virtue in her, nor ever was. All her experiences of the presence of God now seem to her to be a delusion, and she is wracked with anger, sadness and despair (see Angela, 1993, p. 201).

These torments, says Angela, continued for more than two years, at the time seeming to be endless waves of despair. Pride, the constant peril of the spiritual life, surges up to engulf her. Even the virtue she thought she had is now seen as conceit, what we might term the reinforcing of a now discredited ego. Such experiences of desolation seem common among mystics. Just in the last few years, many were surprised by the discovery of diaries of Mother Teresa of Calcutta, which revealed that for years she had felt no joy in prayer or sense of God's presence. St Silouan, a twentieth-century monk on the holy mountain of Athos in Greece, also went through such trials, echoing Angela's wish for hell with his own dictum: 'Keep your mind in hell, but do not despair.' Francis himself seems to have suffered from periods of despair, believing his whole life to have been a failure, though his biographer Thomas of Celano is purposefully vague about this troubled aspect of the saint. At the time, these nights of faith are a darkness with no relief, no purpose that can be discerned; only later are they discovered to be part of the purgation of the soul, a necessary purification of faith. Ultimately, such times of aridity can lead to a more profound illumination and it is to this final step that we now turn.

Finding God in the darkness

In her Seventh Supplementary Step, Angela finds her way to God not so much through the darkness as in the darkness itself. Before, she had seen the light, beauty and fullness that is in God, but all this is taken away from her and she loses the awareness of God's love. Still, God is there, but in a wholly different way:

After that, I saw God in a darkness – in a darkness because God is a greater good than can be conceived or understood; in fact, nothing that can be conceived or understood touches or even approaches that goodness. Then my soul was given a very certain faith, a secure and very firm hope, and a constant certainty about God, which has taken away all fear from me.

And in this good which is seen in the darkness I was completely reconciled. (Mazzoni, 1999, pp. 67–8)

Startlingly, the one who was so full of love and joy now describes herself as 'nonlove'. This is a mysterious transition, what might be called discovering 'the treasures of darkness' (Isa. 45.3). And yet it is still good; in fact it is a more secure good than any she has so far experienced:

No matter how far the soul or heart expands itself, all that expanse is less than this good. What I related until now – that is when the soul sees all creation overflowing with God's presence, when it sees the divine power or the divine wisdom – all this is inferior to this most secret good, because this good which I see with darkness is the whole, and all other things are but parts. (Angela, 1993, p. 203)

This experience of God in the darkness brings no smile to her lips, nor warmth to her heart. What Angela seems to be experiencing here is the transition from the *Via Positiva* to the *Via Negativa*, from the Way of Light to the Way of Darkness, which was the experience of many of the Franciscan saints. It is also known as the apophatic path, that is, to move away from the use of language to define God, tending rather to silence in the contemplation of divinity. It is an approach to theology that suggests it is impossible to say accurately what God is, only what God is not. It's a bit like the difference between oil painting and sculpture. In oil painting, layers of colour and texture are built up to create a picture on an initially blank canvas; in sculpture, whether wood or stone, all that is not needed is chipped away from an original block – the work is in removing what is not required. So kataphatic theology builds up an image of God, whereas apophatic theology removes all superfluous discourse about God and tends towards 'knowing by unknowing' (see Williams, 2018, pp. 52–60). This latter movement in the spiritual life has a venerable tradition, going back at least as far as Gregory of Nyssa (c. 330–c. 395). In his work *The Life of Moses*, Gregory writes about Moses' ascent of Mount Sinai:

> What does it mean that Moses entered the darkness and then saw God in it? What is now recounted seems somehow to be contradictory to the first theophany [at the burning bush], for then the Divine was beheld in light but now he is seen in darkness. (Gregory, 1978, pp. 94–5)

For Gregory, the revelation of God in darkness surpasses the revelation of light. This is a way of 'seeing that consists in not seeing, knowing by unknowing', because whatever can ordinarily be seen and known is far beneath the infinite and incomprehensible nature of God. In fourteenth-century England, the anonymous author of *The Cloud of Unknowing* was deeply influenced by this understanding of the spiritual path. The author writes:

> But now you will ask me, 'How am I to think of God himself, and what is he?' and I cannot answer you except to say, 'I do not know!' For with this question you have brought me into the same darkness, the same cloud of unknowing where I want you to be! (*Cloud*, 1961, p. 59)

It is this mind of 'not knowing' that is the way to God. This is by no means a casual agnosticism that believes nothing can be known about God so the whole issue should simply be forgotten. Rather this is an intense search for the true God beyond all images, using the question 'What is God?' or 'What is Love?', or just the single word 'God', 'Love', or 'Jesus' as an arrow of longing love fired into the depths of an unseen God. The name of God alone becomes a focus to drive out all distractions, putting all else apart from this fundamental quest under a 'cloud of forgetting'. When this search matures, it leads to a certainty that is beyond all theological abstraction, all intellectual doubt. It is a state of great simplicity, the union of the soul with God. Angela writes:

When I am in that darkness I do not remember anything about humanity or the God-man, or anything that has form. Yet when I am in that darkness I see everything and I see nothing. And as I depart from what I have been talking about (or as I remain behind), I see the God-man. He draws my soul with such gentleness, and he sometimes says, 'You are I and I am you.' (Mazzoni, 1999, p. 69)

Now this is dangerous territory. People have been burnt at the stake for saying less and some of Angela's contemporaries did indeed lose their lives at the hands of the Inquisition. In essence, the experience Angela describes is an expression of St Paul's saying: 'I have been crucified with Christ; and it is no longer I who live, but it is Christ who lives in me' (Gal. 2.19–20), a verse much beloved of Christian mystics. Or as Paul says elsewhere: 'But anyone united to the Lord becomes one spirit with him' (1 Cor. 6.17). This experience leads to an all-encompassing equanimity, as Angela goes on to say:

And although at times I can experience small sorrows and joys externally, nevertheless there is a room within my soul where no entrance is made by any joy or sorrow, or even by the delight of any virtue or of anything that can be named. But there in that room is the All-Good, which is not another good, or rather it is so completely good that there is no other good … I also see the One who is Being and I see how he is the Being of all creatures. (Mazzoni, 1999, p. 75)

Here God is found as the All Good fully present in every lesser good, as Being Itself holding all things in being, the One Who Is. Angela discovers this All Good in a chamber of her soul, into which only God, the Being of all creatures, can enter. And yet she is not thereby isolated from the rest of creation. The One who is her Being is the Being of all things, the irrepressible Good at the heart of everything that breathes, the ever-flowing delight that knows no separation or boundary in all the created world.

In his German sermons, the Dominican friar Meister Eckhart (c. 1260–c. 1328) speaks of this mystery as 'the citadel in the soul', picking up Angela's description of the secret chamber of her soul and, it seems, taking the analogy to an even further level:

> So unified is the 'citadel' in the soul, of which I speak and to which I am referring, above all manners and modes, that that noble power of which I have spoken [the spark of the soul] is not worthy to peep into this citadel even once, for a split second. Even that other power, of which I spoke, and in which God glows and burns with all his wealth and with all his bliss, never dares to peer in there. So entirely one and simple is this citadel, and so far above all particular manner and all powers is this single oneness, that no power or manner can ever look into it, not even God himself. (Eckhart, 1994, p. 163)

Even the Trinity cannot enter into this sacred space of infinite Being, this Oneness beyond all differentiation. To understand further this revelation of God in the heart and mind we will turn next to another Franciscan mystic, the poet Jacopone da Todi. But before we turn the page, Angela must have the final word as she recounts an experience one Wednesday of Holy Week, seeking to empty herself to be more receptive to the Son of God in his Passion:

> Suddenly, while I was engrossed in this effort and desire, a divine word sounded in my soul: 'My love for you has not been a hoax.' These words struck me a mortal blow. For immediately the eyes of my soul were opened and I saw that what he had said was true. I saw his acts of love, everything that the Son of God had done, all that he had endured in life and in death – this suffering God-man – because of his inexpressible and visceral love. Seeing in him all the deeds of true love, I understood the perfect truth of what he had said, that his love for me had not been a hoax, but that he had

loved me with a most perfect and visceral love. I saw, on the other hand, the exact opposite in myself, because my love for him had never been anything but playing games, never true. Being made aware of this was a mortal blow and caused such intolerable pain that I thought I would die ...

I perceived all the signs and marks of the truest love in him; how he had given himself wholly and totally to me, in order to serve me; how he had come so close to me: he had become human in order to truly feel and carry my sufferings in himself. When, on the other hand, I perceived the exact opposite in me, I had such suffering and pain that I thought I would die. I felt my ribs dislocate in my chest under the weight of my pain, and it seemed as though my heart would burst. (Angela, 1993, pp. 280–1)

7

The Poet: Jacopone da Todi
(c. 1230–1306)

Jacopone dei Benedetti was born in Todi some time in the 1230s. He entered this life as a fortunate child, if only because he survived at a time when infant mortality was so high. Illness and death were all around him and they were often the subject of his anguished verse. The fact that he was able to study and learn Latin was an indication of his privileged background. He even went on to qualify as a lawyer: a sure route to wealth and success. In the end, fame came to him as a mystical poet, writing in his native Umbrian dialect. Bernard McGinn says of him: 'His *Lauds* are astonishing in their range and their complexity of tone and message … Jacopone's ability to suggest the annihilating power of the experience of divine love has few rivals in the history of Christian mysticism' (McGinn, 1998, p. 126).

But Jacopone never lost sight of 'The Pain of Living', as he called it in one of his early poems, or 'Lauds' (that is 'songs') as they are usually called. Whether or not he is writing autobiographically, in Laud 24 Jacopone writes in biting terms of the suffering inherent in all lives:

> If mother should come and tell the trouble she had in feeding me! She had to get up at night and give me the breast, suffering with cold and standing at her service, and I was crying. I had no reason to cry. She, thinking that I was sick and might die, trembled all over; she had to light a light to see me, and then she examined me and found no reason for my crying – why it should have been. (Peck, 1980, p. 135)

Then came the time when my father was moved to put me to learning to read and write; if I didn't learn what was put in front of me, he gave me a big beating as a reward; with what fear I stayed there would be too long to tell. (Peck, 1980, p. 3)

Jacopone is acutely aware of the sufferings of daily life; childhood and parenthood are described unflinchingly, with a keen sense of the pains and anxieties that are the normal experience of life. Like Francis, he seems to be closer to his mother than his father, more aware of the intrinsic suffering of women in bearing and raising a child. But it doesn't end there – young adulthood brings its own temptations and troubles:

As time passed, I took to gambling, going about in society, and making great expenditures. My father mourned over it and would not pay for my bad activities; the expenses I incurred forced me to steal, and I wasted the harvest in a bad way. (Peck, 1980, p. 29)

Jacopone's extravagant youth sounds like that of Francis, as described by his biographer Thomas of Celano:

[Francis] had been the ringleader of Assisi's frivolous young crowd. They still invited him to their dinner parties, in which the suggestive and vulgar were always served. They chose him as their leader, since they had often experienced his generosity, and knew for sure he would pay all their expenses. (*FA:ED*, vol. 2, p. 246)

This description may be something of an exaggeration. There was a tendency in hagiography, the recording of the lives of the saints, to paint a harsh picture of a misspent youth so as to highlight the extent of the saint's later conversion. This account by Thomas is rather harder on Francis than his earlier telling of the story in his first *Life of St Francis of Assisi*. In that earlier account, there is reference to a wistful longing, even as a young man, for something more exalted than his current life. Some thought that he was in love:

People thought he wanted to get married, and they would ask him: 'Do you want to get married, Francis?' He replied: 'I will take a bride more noble and more beautiful than you have ever seen, and she will surpass the rest in beauty and excel all others in wisdom.' (*FA:ED*, vol. 1, p. 188)

The bride he is talking about is Lady Poverty, as becomes clear later in the story. In this way, Francis is adapting the ideal of courtly love, as if he were a knight enamoured not of an unattainable beloved, but of poverty itself.

Jacopone also dreamed of love, but at this stage in his life he was still in the sphere of the mundane and had rather a long list of requirements:

I wanted for my pleasure a beautiful wife who was healthy and not vain – with a large dowry, kind and even tempered, from a family that was not foreign, with a ready tongue. (Peck, 1980, p. 7)

Francis never married and instead took the vows of poverty, chastity and obedience. Jacopone, however, seems to have found the woman of his dreams. At about the age of 30 he married Donna Vanna, daughter of a noble family, rich and beautiful. A verse from another laud seems to be a reminiscence of his wife:

I remember a woman who was white and rosy, beautifully dressed and soft – she was a marvel. The thought of her lovely ways torments me; I should like so much to speak with her. (Peck, 1980, p. 7)

According to a contemporary Franciscan biography, Jacopone used to take great delight in seeing his wife dressed in all the latest fashions, even though she wanted to live a simpler life. But then disaster struck. One day when Vanna was at a party, dancing to the music, the balcony on which she stood collapsed and she was crushed by the falling debris. Jacopone raced to the scene and, gathering up the limp body of his beloved, carried her back to their home. There, as she was being undressed to prepare her body for burial, Vanna was found to be wearing a coarse hair shirt next to her skin underneath her rich finery. Such garments were designed to irritate the skin as a penitential practice to expiate sins. Her husband had no idea that she had lived a secretly devout life and the knowledge of how little he had really known her, and the loss of his beloved so young, nearly drove Jacopone out of his mind.

The Penitent

From then on, Jacopone found all his previous dreams to be an exercise in vanity. He gave his possessions away to the poor and, like Francis, exchanged his fine clothes for the garb of a hermit, taking up the life of a wandering penitent. It is a moot question whether he was reacting out of grief for the loss of his wife, or if it was revulsion at his own vacuous life that most unhinged him. In any case, he became a chastened man, and for the next ten years he lived at the very edge of society, frequently offending the townspeople of Todi by the extravagance of his penitential practices and by his condemnation of all that he now saw as culpable vanity. In particular, he was obsessed by the thought of death. In Laud 25 – 'On the Contemplation of Death and the Burning Away of Pride' – Jacopone presents a dialogue between the living and the dead, as a kind of macabre duet. The translation of Mrs Theodore Beck, used by Evelyn Underhill in her study of Jacopone, reflects the rhyming structure of the original Umbrian Italian verse, and adds an ironic note of jauntiness to the sombre subject matter:

> When you are merry, and your head is high,
> Think on the grave, O mortal, where you must lie.
>
> Come here, your sepulchre to contemplate,
> And think, you too must share this heavy fate;
> Like his in this dark ditch shall be your state,
> You too must bear the grave's indignity.

Now answer me, O mortal, entombed and dead,
You who so swiftly from this world have sped;
Where are your clothes, once bright with gold and red?
I see you here adorned so loathsomely.
(Underhill, 1919, p. 269)

The full poem is a gruesome litany of the depredations of death. Slowly but thoroughly, the living man interrogates the deceased, asking where his fine clothing, his well-groomed hair, his clear eyes, his proud nose, his razor-sharp tongue have all gone. What is left of the lips that both smiled and mocked, the arms that were once so strong, the property that once promised a comfortable life? Poems like this were set to music and sung by wandering bands of penitents, calling out to people to renounce their sins and prepare to meet their maker. Jacopone ends with a solemn warning:

Now look on me, O man of worldly mind;
No longer in this world your pleasures find;
For step by step, take care, fool and blind!
You will be bound and shackled cruelly!
(Underhill, 1919, p. 273)

It was not unknown for Francis himself to challenge people about their fragile confidence in their longevity. In his *Later Admonition and Exhortation to the Brothers and Sisters of Penance*, Francis writes:

You think you possess the vanities of the world for a long time, but you are deceived because a day and an hour are coming of which you do not think, do not know, and are not aware. The body becomes weak, death approaches, relatives and friends come saying: 'Put your affairs in order.' (*FA:ED*, vol. 1, pp. 50–1)

Francis goes on to warn against entrusting your fate to the hands of your family, for who can be saved from the judgement of God? In one of his prophetic signs, an acted parable of a sermon, Francis once showed the sisters at San Damiano how we are all dust and ashes in the end:

> The Ladies gathered as usual to hear the word of God, but no less to see their father, and he raised his eyes to heaven, where he always had his heart, and began to pray to Christ. Then he had ashes brought and made a circle with them round himself on the floor, and then put the rest on his own head. As they waited, the blessed father remained in silence within the circle of ashes, and real amazement grew in their hearts. Suddenly he got up, and to their great surprise, recited the 'Have mercy on me, God,' instead of a sermon. As he finished it, he left quickly. The hand-maids of God were so filled with contrition by the power of this mime that they were flowing with tears. (*FA:ED*, vol. 2, pp. 379–80)

The 'Have mercy on me, God' is Psalm 51, which would have been widely memorized by religious, and chanted at least once a day as part of the Divine Office. At other times of day, it would have been used as a kind of extended mantra, to keep the mind from idle thoughts. This psalm is one of the 'seven penitential psalms', recited by heart as part of a penitential discipline, especially during the season of Lent. Francis lived an almost perpetual Lent, except on Christmas Day, when he said all creatures should rejoice and be well fed.

For Jacopone, however, penitence is not necessarily negative. It can be a means of transforming sorrow into joy. He says in Laud 4:

> Lofty penitence, suffering endured for love's sake,
> You are precious indeed, for through you heaven is won.
> Not imposed from without, but embraced by my will,
> I forge you into joy. To the well-ordered soul
> The only real suffering is sin;
> All other pain is joy in potency.
> (Jacopone, 1982, p. 75)

Penitence is like bitter medicine for the soul – it tastes sour in the mouth, but ultimately brings health and spiritual well-being. Jacopone throws himself into penitence with all his powers of eloquence and imagination in Laud 48 – 'The Ills and Evils Frate Jacopone Called Down on Himself in an Excess of Charity':

> Send me illness, O Lord,
> I beg of you, out of courtesy!
>
> Hurl down quartian ague, tertian fever,
> Chills every day and swollen dropsy!
> Give me toothache, headache, and stomach cramps,
> Pains in my guts and spasms of choking.
> Give me pleuritis and burning eyes,
> Let my left side swell with a tumour;
> Visit me with a violent case of tuberculosis,
> Let me suffer perpetual delirium ...
>
> All this I call down on myself, O Lord, is not adequate
>   vengeance,
> For you created me as your beloved,
> And I, ungrateful wretch, put you to death.
> (Jacopone, 1982, pp. 164–5)

It is an outrageous poem, as Jacopone calls down every disease and malady upon himself, as if he were using a medical textbook as a mail-order catalogue. If this extract seems excessive then read the remaining stanzas (not printed here), where he really does get a little carried away. He redeems himself just enough by the last three lines, where the reader suddenly realizes why he is calling down all these calamities on his trembling body. But there is just a hint in the very language itself that Jacopone is actually rather enjoying his eloquence, his command of the situation in which he is overtly surrendering all control. It is reminiscent of the beautiful sonnet by the sixteenth-century English poet John Donne:

Batter my heart, three-person'd God, for you
As yet but knock, breathe, shine, and seek to mend;
That I may rise and stand, o'erthrow me, and bend
Your force to break, blow, burn, and make me new.
I, like an usurp'd town to another due,
Labour to admit you, but oh, to no end;
Reason, your viceroy in me, me should defend,
But is captiv'd, and proves weak or untrue.
Yet dearly I love you, and would be lov'd fain,
But am betroth'd unto your enemy;
Divorce me, untie or break that knot again,
Take me to you, imprison me, for I,
Except you enthrall me, never shall be free,
Nor ever chaste, except you ravish me.
(John Donne, 1572–1631)

Donne also revels in his poetic skills, and yet invites the reader into the question of what it really is to be confronted with the living God. Can we really see the face of God and live? Donne wants God to truly break through his defences and carry him off, like the *raptus*, the rapture of mystical prayer, that we have seen in the writings of so many medieval Franciscans.

Hypocrisy unmasked

What really offends Jacopone is the hypocrisy he sees both in himself and in others, particularly members of his own Franciscan Order. After ten years as an independent hermit, he managed to persuade the friars in his home town of Todi to accept him as a member of their community. One wonders if they knew what they were letting themselves in for; perhaps they thought it safer to have him inside the Order where there might just be a controlled outlet for his rampant spiritual energies.

Francis himself was, of course, something of a force to be reckoned with and one who was as critical of himself as he was of others.

> Once at the hermitage of Poggio about the time of the Lord's nativity a large crowd assembled for the sermon, which [Francis] began with this opening: 'You all believe me to be a holy man, and that is why you came to me with great devotion. But I declare to you that this whole Lent I have eaten food flavoured with lard.' In this way he often blamed pleasure for what was, in fact, a concession to illness.
>
> With the same fervour, whenever his spirit was moved to vanity, he displayed it naked before everyone with a confession. Once as he was going through the city of Assisi, an old woman met him and asked him for something. As he had nothing except his mantle, he offered it with quick generosity. But then he felt an impulse of empty congratulations, and at once he confessed before everyone that he felt vainglory. (*FA:ED*, vol. 2, pp. 334–5)

Doing the right thing for the wrong reason, as T. S. Eliot has Thomas Becket say before he embraces martyrdom, is a dangerous pitfall in the spiritual life, 'the greatest treason'. Humility is the key, but that virtue is so difficult to attain, as the moment you are praised for humility the virtue is lost and you are back to square one. Hypocrisy is the corruption of assumed humility and is really an aspect of pride. Jacopone explains more in his Laud 29:

> I have strayed from the path trodden by the saints,
> Strayed far, twisting my way into hypocrisy.
> People consider me one of the illuminated,
> And so I seem on the surface, as if humility dwelt in my heart;
> But refuse me honour, and watch me sulk!
> The man who has faith in me, in him I delight.
> (Jacopone, 1982, pp. 120–1)

He goes on to boast of the pleasure he gets in displaying his virtues, pretending to flee the company of others in order to pray when it is really a ruse to avoid criticism to his face. The archetypal wolf in sheep's clothing, he enjoys the adulation he gets for the mere look of a feigned asceticism, when in reality he is hungry for praise, not for God. It is possible that Jacopone is here speaking of other seemingly holy friars, but the edge of the criticism seems much more likely to be aimed at himself. He is clearly aware of the pitfalls of religion and how easy it is to deceive oneself as to the motivations by which one acts.

Both Francis and Jacopone had an acute sense of the failings of the institutional Church. Francis, though he was intensely loyal to the Church, recognized the need for reform. In particular, he acknowledged the need for trained ministers of the word, though he emphasized that the preparation to preach should be more by prayer than by study. It was undeniable that the 'secular' clergy, that is, those appointed as diocesan priests, rarely had the ability to preach well. That was why preaching was such a central activity for the friars. Nevertheless, Francis criticized those learned friars who thought they were doing great things by their preaching:

> He felt deeply sorry for those preachers who often sell what they do for the price of some empty praise. He would sometimes treat the swelling of such people with this antidote: 'Why do you boast about people being converted? My simple brothers converted them by their prayers!' (*FA:ED*, vol. 2, pp. 352–3)

True preachers, Francis wrote, first grow warm with their hearts full of devotion, otherwise their words will be frozen on the outside. Better still, all should preach by their actions rather than by their words. The true 'knights of the round table', Francis once said, are the brothers praying in obscurity in the hermitages in the hills, not the preachers gathering great crowds in the cities, impressed by their learning (*FA:ED*, vol. 2, p. 208).

This tension between those who study and those who simply pray is deeply felt by Jacopone. He would not have agreed with the arguments put forward by Bonaventure as to the nature of theology and its importance in a Franciscan life. Rather, like Giles in an earlier generation, Jacopone lamented what he saw as the corruption of Assisi by the lecture halls of Paris. Laud 31 – 'How Ambition and Idle Knowledge Destroy the Purity of the Rule' – is biting in its critical contempt, brought out by Peck's unadorned prose translation:

> So it is; there is no more religion. We see Paris as bad; it has destroyed Assisi; it has set it on the bad way with its learning.
>
> Whoever follows learning goes abroad; the rest stay in the refectory to eat greens with oil. If the lector loses his appetite, he is served like an emperor; if the cook falls sick, no one goes to see him. They gather in the chapter to make many regulations; the first to propose them is the first to break them. See the great love they have for each other in their hearts! (Peck, 1980, p. 102)

Jacopone complains that self-interest is the curriculum of the universities and rivalry the accepted path to preferment. And the theologians are dangerous too – disagree with them in debate and you will find yourself posted to a run-down friary far away from home. All this closely mirrors the criticisms made by Brother Giles, as we saw in an earlier chapter, and bears testimony to an undercurrent of unease among some of the brothers concerning the development of the Order.

Sometimes the rhetoric gets up close and personal. You can imagine the other friars being wary of Jacopone's tongue. Who would dare sit next to him in the friary refectory? He lets no one off the hook, living or dead, as seen in his 'eulogy' in Laud 17 for the late Brother Rinaldo:

> Brother Rinaldo, where have you gone?
> And what philosophical points
> Have you made of late?

Tell me, Brother Rinaldo, for I'm not sure
Whether or not you've paid your debts.
Are you in glory or is it warmer there?
(Jacopone, 1982, p. 98)

Jacopone taunts Rinaldo, warning him that the honour of his
qualifications is not so useful after all. Now he is to be judged
by Truth, not by the cleverness of his debating techniques.
Sophisms and syllogisms are of no use to him now as he faces
his final exam. In life, did he really rejoice in being poor and
despised, as all good Franciscans should, at least according to
Francis and Jacopone? Or did he rather enjoy his status and
the power that came with an expensive education?

Spouses of our Lord Jesus Christ

Having read thus far, the reader may think that Jacopone is
little more than a cantankerous old man, criticizing all the
many abuses of power around him and denouncing others at
every opportunity. But there is another side to Jacopone, one
that is saturated with the love of God. Sometimes it is shown
in rather didactic fashion, as the friar enumerates aspects of
the spiritual path. One such occasion is Laud 45 – 'The Five
Ways in which God Reveals Himself', in which Jacopone lists
the ways the Lord appears to him as fear, healing love, tender
sustenance, fatherly affection and finally by the love of a bridegroom to the soul. He then goes on to describe each of the
modes of love in turn. The first stage is the putting to flight of
the demons within, being released by contrition. The second is
the visitation by the Healer, restoring the soul through forgiveness and strengthening it through the sacraments. Then comes
Love as a companion, endowing the soul with virtues. Fourth
is the approach of God as a gentle father in great generosity.
In all these ways God speaks tenderly to the soul, with reassur-
ance rather than criticism. But it is the fifth mode that catches
the ear in a way that has not been disclosed so far in his poetry:

In the fifth mode Love leads me to the conjugal bed
And I lie in the embrace of the Son of God. O my soul,
Led by grace, you are the queen of the angels,
In wondrous fusion transformed into Christ.
(Jacopone, 1982, p. 158)

This is a different, so far unsounded note, one that once more
echoes the book beloved of mystical writers – Solomon's Song
of Songs. It is an approach classically and startlingly enunciated
in Laud 42 – 'The Soul Begs the Angels to Help Her Find Christ':

Open, open, I beseech you,
That I might see Christ, in whom I place my hope.
Answer, my Love, my Life, hide yourself no longer.

Soul, since you have come to me,
Gladly will I answer you. Come,
See, this is my bed – the cross.
Here we will be one. Come to me
And I will quench your thirst.

O my Love, naked will I scale that cross,
To suffer and die with you.
Lord, clasped close in your embrace,
In joy will I suffer and die.
(Jacopone, 1982, pp. 145–6)

In his writings, Francis is rarely this explicit in his description
of the unification of the soul and Christ. The nearest he gets is
in his *Later Admonition and Exhortation to the Brothers and
Sisters of Penance*, where he writes: '[We] are spouses, brothers
and mothers of our Lord Jesus Christ. We are spouses when
the faithful soul is united by the Holy Spirit to our Lord Jesus
Christ ... O how holy, consoling, beautiful and wonderful to
have such a Spouse!' (*FA:ED*, vol. 1, p. 49). In this, Francis is
echoing the teaching of St Paul, who compared the love of a
husband for his wife to the love of Christ for the Church (Eph.
5.31–32).

In his *Earlier Rule*, however, we do get an inkling of the passion in Francis' soul:

> With our whole heart, our whole soul, our whole mind, with our whole strength and fortitude, with our whole understanding, with all our powers, with every effort, every affection, every feeling, every desire and wish, let us all love the Lord God who has given and gives to each one of us our whole body, our whole soul and our whole life; who has created, redeemed and will save us by his mercy alone. (*FA:ED*, vol. 1, p. 84)

Although this document is described as a rule, in fact it was never accepted as juridical by the Holy See and is therefore known as the *Regula non bullata*, the unauthorized rule. The whole of the final section of the *Earlier Rule* consists of a long flowing prayer written by Francis, which is certainly inspiring but lacking in the rather more dry legislative style required by the church authorities for a legal document. Nonetheless, this passage shows the essential connection for Francis between the love of God, the creation and the incarnation and redemptive death of Christ. The prayer and thanksgiving quoted above is preceded by an extended 'Admonition to the Brothers', which itself begins with a thanksgiving for the loving self-sacrifice of Christ.

Jacopone himself acknowledges that he is following in the footsteps of Francis by their shared devotion to Christ on the cross as he says in Laud 61 – 'Saint Francis and the Seven Visions of the Cross'. As Jacopone explains, it was not so much in words as in the physical transformation of his body into the image of the crucified Christ that Francis demonstrated his love. Clare's language about becoming the bride of Christ, as found in her letters to Agnes of Prague, captures more of the feel of such devotion in words, but it is Francis who sealed his devotion with the whole of his body as he received the wounds of Christ.

Poverty and joy

As well as being united in their love of Christ crucified, Francis,
Clare and Jacopone find common ground in their attitude to
poverty. This was a quintessential virtue in the Franciscan
movement, perhaps most clearly embodied in the writings of
Clare, but taken to a new metaphysical level by Jacopone, as
seen in Laud 60 – 'Holy Poverty and its Threefold Heaven'.
Here the mundane experience of grinding poverty 'is an
overcast sky', whereas the heavenly form of freely-embraced
poverty is like the third heaven to which Paul ascended (2 Cor.
12.2), full of the presence of God:

> The name of this heaven is Nonbeing –
> All affirmations are forbidden
> There where Love is a prisoner
> In that dark light.
>
> All light is shrouded in darkness,
> All darkness bright as the noonday sun;
> This new philosophy
> Has burst the old wineskins.
>
> Where Christ enters in, the old world is swept away,
> Lover and beloved are fused in a wondrous union.
> Love no longer needs the heart,
> Nor knowledge the intelligence – our will is his.
>
> To live as myself and yet not I,
> My being no longer my being,
> This is a paradox
> We cannot pretend to understand!
>
> Poverty is having nothing, wanting nothing,
> And possessing all things in the spirit of freedom.
> (Jacopone, 1982, p. 186)

Jacopone alludes to Paul's famous charter of the abandonment of self in God: 'I have been crucified with Christ; and it is no longer I who live, but it is Christ who lives in me' (Gal. 2.19–20). Jacopone goes on to talk about this heaven in negative terms – the *via negativa*. In this path, all affirmations regarding God are relinquished and all that can be achieved by words is a description of what God is not. Thus, the knowledge of God is built on 'non-being' (*nihil*): not that God is literally nothing, but that nothing can contain or express God, who is known by 'unknowing', whose light is darkness to our eyes. This, for Jacopone, is the true meaning of poverty: having nothing, and yet possessing all things (2 Cor. 6.10).

And this poverty leads to great joy, as in Laud 76: 'On the Heart's Jubilation'. Here Jacopone's heart sings with joy, uncontrollably, blissfully unaware of anything less than the exaltation that he feels:

> O jubilant joy and somersaults of happiness,
> Pray, learn to be prudent:
> Sensible people with sensible smiles
> Cannot understand the wildness of your ecstasy!
> (Jacopone, 1982, p. 228)

Francis would surely have enjoyed this song, perhaps dancing a jig with Jacopone, two wild friars having a ball:

> Blessed Francis had this as his highest and main goal: he was always careful to have and preserve in himself spiritual joy internally and externally, even though from the beginning of his conversion until the day of his death he greatly afflicted his body. He used to say that if a servant of God always strives to have and preserve joy internally and externally which proceeds from purity of heart, the devils can do him no harm. They would say: 'Since the servant of God has joy both in tribulation and in prosperity, we do not know where to find an entrance to enter him and do him harm.' (*FA:ED*, vol. 2, pp. 229–30)

Francis always wanted the brothers around him to keep a cheerful countenance and not to look glum. If they had sinned, they should sort it out with God; if not, they should smile (*FA:ED*, vol. 2, p. 230). On one occasion, when Francis was trying to give a sermon but was drowned out by a braying donkey, the noisy beast soon calmed down at his rebuke, but to distract the crowd from this uncanny control over nature, Francis reeled off a series of jokes about the donkey and made everyone laugh (Habig, 1972, p. 1882).

A jail-bird sings

Francis and Jacopone were not just companions in revels: they were both involved in criticism of the secular and religious rulers of their respective times. In the early days of the Brothers' life together with Francis, there is a curious incident of prophecy that took place on the road past Assisi:

> At that time the emperor Otto passed through that area, travelling in great pomp and circumstance to receive the crown of an earthly empire. The most holy father [Francis] and his followers were staying in that small hut next to the very parade route. He did not go outside to look and did not allow the others to do so, except for one who, without wavering, proclaimed to the emperor that his glory would be short-lived ... Apostolic authority resided in him; so he altogether refused to flatter kings and princes. (*FA:ED*, vol. 1, p. 221)

Jacopone's run-in with authority was rather more serious and long lasting. On the election of Pope Boniface VIII, Jacopone signed a letter denouncing the new pope for the laxity of his morals and doubting the validity of his election. Boniface had replaced the saintly but ineffectual Pope Celestine, who had been a keen supporter of the more radical Franciscans, allowing them to observe the Rule as literally as possible. Previously a hermit, Celestine was not prepared for the cut and thrust of ecclesiastical politics and resigned soon after his election. Once Boniface was on the papal throne, Celestine all too conveniently died, having already been imprisoned, leaving his corrupt successor free to act without censure. Some, however, did actively challenge Boniface, including the cardinals from Colonna and the friar Jacopone. They ended up taking refuge in the Palestrina fortress, finally having to surrender and be led away in chains. Jacopone spent the next several years in prison, in a friary dungeon, from which came some of his most bitter Lauds. Here is a part of Laud 55 – 'The Canticle of Brother Jacopone in Prison':

What will you do, Fra Jacopone? You have come to your trial ...
As a prebendary of the court of Rome, this has been my reward; All my fame has been darkened, such has been my curse. I have got my living and my cowl has been taken from me, imprisoned forever, chained like a lion.

The prison that has been given me is an underground cell; there is an open latrine that does not smell of musk. No one may speak with me except the jailer, but he must report all I say.

I wear as scourges the leather straps that hawks have on their talons; they jingle when I walk; whoever is near my perch can hear a new dance. When I lie down and then turn over, I find my legs confined in irons, kneaded by the chains. I wear a rope belt that is not repulsive to the rats. My cell could hold, by my calculation, five loaves of bread.
(Peck, 1980, pp. 125–6)

Gradually, as he seemed to give up hope of being released, the songs that he sang in that fetid darkness became embittered to the core, as we see in Laud 56 – 'Letter from Jail to Pope Boniface VIII'. The sing-song lyrics sound like a child's taunt in a playground, though the situation is far from the innocence of youth. Jacopone still defers to the pope's right to excom-

municate and reconcile a penitent at will, but the hope that he
will absolve in this case is fading fast.

> O Boniface, you who are pope,
> Your ban is heavy on my hope;
> Your malediction and your hate
> Have made me excommunicate.
>
> Your forky tongue, so like a snake's,
> This wound upon my spirit makes:
> There let your tongue again be laid,
> To staunch the hurt itself has made.
>
> No other power but yours can heal
> This gaping wound I still must feel;
> None other can my griefs dispel;
> If you absolve me, I am well.
>
> By God's dear grace I humbly pray,
> Speak but the words '*Absolvo te*':
> All else I'll bear with steadfast mind,
> Until I leave the world behind.
> (Underhill, 1919, p. 439)

Perhaps it was during this time in prison that Jacopone, natur-
ally enough, felt abandoned by the love of God. His songs of
lament are sad gestures of despair, hurled at a seemingly absent
God. The situation is remarkably similar to that of St John of
the Cross in his Toledo prison 200 years later in Spain; but
the Carmelite friar writes with a lightness of touch about his
dark night and eventual escape. The Franciscan friar Jacopone
writes with a greater sense of despair. One such Laud is 68 –
'The Soul Laments the Disappearance of God':

> Weep, my grieving harrowed soul, for you are widowed by
> the love of Christ. Weep, grieve, and utter sighs, for you have
> lost your sweet Lord. Perhaps by means of my lament, you
> will make it come back to my sad and disconsolate heart.

I wish to weep and I have reason, for I have lost father and husband; fond Christ, flowering lily, has left me because of my fault ...

O my eyes, why do you not weep so much as to lose your sight? You have lost the greatest gift of contemplating pure splendour. O my ears, how can you delight in hearing the lament of the bitter people? Can you not hear the beloved voice that made you sing with joy?

(Peck, 1980, p. 166)

Songs of despair such as this are reminiscent of the songs of love and loss written by the Beguine mystic Hadewijch (thirteenth century). Indeed, in many ways, Jacopone seems to mirror the writings of the Beguines. These were independent groups of holy women who gathered in communities for mutual support in prayer, making a living through the work of their hands. Hadewijch writes:

I do not complain of suffering for Love:
It becomes me always to submit to her,
Whether she commands in storm or in stillness.
One can know her only in herself.
    This is an unconceivable wonder,
    Which has thus filled my heart
And makes me stray in a wild desert.

Never was so cruel a desert created
As Love can make in her land!
For she impels us to long desiringly for her
And to taste her without knowing her being.
    She shows herself as she takes flight;
    We pursue her, but she remains unseen:
This makes the miserable heart ever exert itself.

(Hadewijch, 1980, p. 187)

Both Jacopone and Hadewijch use the conventions of those courtly love poems where the mistress tantalizes her suitor by offering love and then disappears, leaving the lover abandoned as in a desert. Hadewijch complains of Love's cruelty: to her, God is like a paramour playing games with her suitor. Jacopone calls Love a thief of his joy, which is turned to dejection in her wilful absence. In both, the gender balance is reversed: God is the unattainable woman, the soul is the disconsolate man.

Drowning in the abyss of God's love

At this point there is a remarkable turn-around in the corpus of Jacopone's Lauds. Something seems to have happened which turned his world around. Suddenly, his grieving sense of self becomes lost in the ocean of God's love, his understanding emptied out in a vast, silent awe. In three epic poems, Jacopone maps out the denouement of the soul. First, he speaks of the desolation of desire, the longing for God that he finds all-consuming, as he sings in Laud 90: 'The Lament of the Soul for the Intensity of Infused Charity':

> For you, O Love, my heart consumes away,
>   I cry, I call, I yearn for your caress;
> Living, I perish when you do not stay,
>   Sighing and mourning for my Blessedness:
> If you return, I strain and strive and pray,
>   To lose amidst your All my Nothingness:
>   Then don't delay to bless,
>   Love, think on me;
>   Bind me to be
>   Consumed, my heart, with Love! ...

> I once could speak, but now my lips are dumb;
>   My eyes are blind, although I once could see:
> In this abyss my soul is stark and numb,
>   Silent, I speak; cling, yet am held:
> Falling, I rise; I go, and yet I come:

Pursue, and am pursued; I am bound yet free;
O Love that overwhelms me!
  Maddened I cry:
  'Why must I die,
Your fiery strength to prove?'
(Underhill, 1919, pp. 371–3)

As the title suggests, the poem is a lament; but this time it is not
for the absence of Love, but for the soul that is imprisoned by
Love, with no hope of escape. All has been given up to Love,
and like iron in a blacksmith's fire, no differentiation between
lover and beloved can be made. This is the embrace of Christ,
becoming one body, one soul. It leads to a cascade of coinci-
dent opposites: silent but speaking, fleeing yet bound. The poet
doesn't know which way to turn as every way is the way to
God, and that God is a consuming fire (Heb. 12.29).

Finally, the Laud becomes an overflowing chant as Jacopone,
like a Muslim Sufi engaged in *dhikr*, the recitation of the
sacred names of God, is lost in the embrace of the Name as he
surrenders to the overwhelming love of God.

Love, Love, O Love, the world's wild voices cry,
  Love, Love, O Love, the clamorous echoes spread;
Love, Love, O Love, so deep your treasures lie,
  We hunger more, the more we taste your bread:
Love, Love, O Love, O circling mystery,
  Who enters you at Love's deep heart is fed;
You're loom, and cloth, and thread:
    O sweet to be
    Clothed and set free
  And ceaseless chant of Love.

Love, Love, O Love, your touch so quickens me,
  Love, Love, O Love, I am no longer I:
Love, Love, O Love, yourself so utterly
  You give me, Jesu, that I can but die.
O Love, O Love, you have ravished me,

Love, Love, my Love, with longing I sigh!
  O Love, my bliss!
  O Lover's kiss!
  O quench my soul in Love!
(Underhill, 1919, pp. 382–3)

Irresistibly, the fire of God consumes all that it confronts, which leads ineluctably to Laud 91: 'Self-Annihilation and Charity Lead the Soul to What Lies Beyond Knowledge and Language'.

As air becomes the medium for light when the sun rises,
And as wax melts from the heat of fire,
So the soul drawn to that light is resplendent,
Feels self melt away,
Its will and actions no longer its own.
So clear is the imprint of God
That the soul, conquered, is conqueror;
Annihilated, it lives in triumph.

What happens to the drop of wine
That you pour into the sea?
Does it remain itself, unchanged?
It is as if it never existed.
So it is with the soul: Love drinks it in,
It is united with Truth,
Its old nature fades away,
It is no longer master of itself.

The soul wills and yet does not will:
Its will belongs to another.
It has eyes only for this beauty;
It no longer seeks to possess, as was its wont –
It lacks the strength to possess such sweetness.
The base of this highest of peaks is founded on *nichil*
Shaped nothingness, made one with the Lord.
(Jacopone, 1982, p. 271)

This is a hymn to 'nothingness', not in the sense of a cold, empty absence of existence or meaning, but in the sense of a raging fire that draws all things into its blazing heat. There, nothing which is not God can endure; there is no thing, no being that could be described as in any way separate from God. God is Being itself, the source of all being. God is like a cosmic black hole, from which nothing can escape, around which a galaxy of stars rotates in an infinitely slow and silent dance.

Jacopone daringly uses the word 'annihilation', *nichilitate* in Latin, comparable to the Sufi term *fanaa* in Arabic. But by that he doesn't mean that something that once existed is snuffed out, like the guttering flame of a candle blown out by a gust of wind. Rather, the soul realizes once and for all that there is no possibility of separation from the eternal God: 'the soul, conquered, is conqueror; annihilated, it lives in triumph.' From one perspective, the soul, like a drop of wine, is absorbed into the sea; from another, the sea is poured into the drop, wine becomes suffused with divinity and bread becomes the engrained love of God.

Language like this may sound strange to our modern ears, but it was not so extreme in medieval teaching. As we have already seen, this is the *via negativa*, taught by the Syrian monk known as Dionysius in his *Mystical Theology*, and experienced by so many in the Franciscan tradition. It is the way to God beyond affirmation and negation, it is a core teaching of *The Book of Angela of Foligno* and a major influence on Bonaventure. In some writers, the desire to transcend the more mundane forms of theological discourse leads to startling expressions that are designed to shake people out of what can be a complacent certainty that there is only one form of the Christian faith. People like Jacopone, or the Dominican friar Meister Eckhart (c. 1260–c. 1328), delight in subverting the usual message from the pulpits, not just to shock the faithful, but to wake people up, to convey a sense of the immense mystery which is God. In one of his German sermons, Eckhart says: 'Now know this: all our perfection and all our blessedness depends upon our breaking through, passing beyond all createdness, all temporality and all being and entering into the ground that is without ground' (Eckhart, 1994, p. 187). This is the Divine Abyss, the God beyond God, the Beginning from which all things emerge as from Nothingness (*creatio ex nihilo*), the Infinite (in Hebrew: *ein sof*) beyond all names. (For more on the apophatic tradition, see the books by Cyprian Consiglio and J. P. Williams listed in the bibliography.)

Another writer contemporary with Jacopone was the Beguine Marguerite Porete (d. 1310). She writes on similar themes, stretching Christian theology to breaking point and beyond:

> It is fitting, says Love, that this Soul be similar to the God-head, for she is transformed into God, says Love, which is why she has retained her true form, which is granted and given to her without beginning from One alone who has always loved her by His goodness.
>
> Ah, Love, says this Soul, the meaning of what is said makes me nothing, and the nothingness of this alone has placed me in an abyss below less than nothingness without measure. And the understanding of my nothingness, says this Soul, has given me the All, and the nothingness of this All, says the Soul, has taken from me prayer, and I pray nothing. (Porete, 1993, p. 128)

For Marguerite, God is known as the 'Farnearness', both far and near at the same time. But primarily, God is Love, who transforms the soul into Love such that there is not the slightest distance between them. This makes the soul 'nothing', and yet this nothingness is simultaneously 'the All' which is God. In this state, the soul cannot pray, because God is not experienced as something other than itself, someone 'out there' to which to pray. God is not an object differentiated from the soul as subject, but both are united in the one Goodness which is Love.

Not everyone agreed. Despite being examined and exonerated by two Dominican theologians, Marguerite was convicted of heresy by the Inquisition and sentenced to death. In the end, the issue was not so much the perceived heresy of her views

as her persistence in promulgating her understanding of the
spiritual life. She refused to burn all the copies of her book,
so the Church decreed that her living body should be burnt as
well.

Jacopone, escaping the censure of the Church, continues to
sing of annihilation where Marguerite Porete had sung of her
own nothingness, as we read in Laud 92, 'How Firm Faith and
Hope Bring One to the Threefold State of Self-Annihilation':

Faith and hope have estranged me from myself,
Struck at my heart, annihilated me.
Within and without I am shattered,
Reduced to nothingness:
This is the fruit of centring my life on love.
I am no longer able to flee or to pursue;
Caught in the swell of the sea
I drown, and my words drown with me!

My speech is silence and shout.
I know where he is hidden, for though I see him not
I recognize the signs of his presence
In every creature that is one with him.
Being and nonbeing I have fused together,
And out of love banished my will with its 'yes' and 'no'.
(Jacopone, 1982, pp. 274–5)

The sea, both in the Scriptures and in Jacopone's Laud, is a
symbol of the primaeval chaos, the face of the deep. It seems
forbidding and yet is full of potential as it is covered by the
brooding wings of the Holy Spirit (Gen. 1.2). It is the place
where the mythical beast Leviathan plays (Ps. 104.25–26). It is
the vast abyss that swallows up any creature of the land that
falls into it, and yet it is populated by its own strange creatures.
To enter this sea, the abyss of God, is a fearful thing, and the
only preparation possible is to strip oneself of all that holds
one back (a theme that often recurs in Jacopone's writings).
Entering the deep, one's separateness is lost and the soul is
dissolved in the vastness of God.

And yet, in the songs of Jacopone, there is always a positive note, a drone or undertone sung beneath the melody, that holds the seeker after God in God's everlasting embrace. The use of the word 'annihilation' is a kind of shock tactic, designed to wake up those slumbering in a complacent faith. Like the commandment of Jesus to eat his flesh and drink his blood, it is designed to startle, but not to dismay. It doesn't signify the end of life, but the beginning of a new day which is always today: a welcome into the new dawn of the resurrection of Christ. No one knows the sequence in which Jacopone composed his Lauds, but in the collection as we have it today it is begun and ended with a hymn to Blessed Mary the mother of Jesus Christ. As a symbol of compassionate bearing with the pain of life, this seems to be an altogether appropriate arrangement. Ultimately, the ocean in which we dissolve is not a dark and terrifying place; it is the ocean of God's love, flooding into every aspect of our being, revealing to us the love that is in Jesus, as Jacopone sings:

> High in that Empyrean,
>   The soul finds treasure so great,
>   No place it has, and no date,
> Nothing for tongue to tell.
> And wonder grows more keen,
>   At the soul, thus re-create,
>   In a new and stronger state,
> Where images cannot dwell,
> Where illusions melt and dispel;
>   It cannot be lost in night,
>   Darkness is turned to light
>   In a love so great and free.
> (Underhill, 1919, p. 491)

Epilogue

Being Franciscan: Following in the Footsteps of St Francis of Assisi

As Francis approached the embrace of Sister Death, he wanted to commend his brothers and sisters to the Lord whom he had faithfully served throughout the short term of his life. The form of the blessing used by Francis, and the narrative as told by his biographers, is based on the blessing of Joseph's sons Ephraim and Manasseh by their grandfather Jacob, as recorded in Genesis 48.8–20. Israel, that is Jacob, cannot see well and asks for the children of Joseph to be brought to him. Affectionately he embraces the children and Joseph arranges them for the formal blessing:

> Joseph took them both, Ephraim in his right hand toward Israel's left, and Manasseh in his left hand toward Israel's right, and brought them near him. But Israel stretched out his right hand and laid it on the head of Ephraim, who was the younger, and his left hand on the head of Manasseh, crossing his hands, for Manasseh was the firstborn. He blessed Joseph, and said,

> 'The God before whom my ancestors Abraham and Isaac walked, the God who has been my shepherd all my life to this day, the angel who has redeemed me from all harm, bless the boys; and in them let my name be perpetuated, and the name of my ancestors Abraham and Isaac; and let them grow into a multitude on the earth.'
> (Gen. 48.13–16)

The story of the blessing by Francis is used in a creative way by several of the early texts preserving sayings and stories about Francis. The earliest of them was *The Life of Saint Francis* by Thomas of Celano. This text was approved by Pope Gregory IX in February 1229, six months after the canonization of Francis (making him officially 'Saint Francis'), and just two years after the death of Francis, in October 1226. It was a work intended to spread the message of Francis and to encourage the laity to follow his example of conversion and renewal in the faith.

At the time of its writing, Brother Elias of Cortona was one of the leading brothers of the Order of Friars Minor, the Order founded by Francis. Pope Gregory gave him responsibility for the temporary housing of the body of Francis until he could begin the task of building a new basilica that would enshrine and keep safe Francis' mortal remains. Elias' high status is evident in the way the story of the blessing is told. The biblical background includes the blessing of Jacob by his father Isaac; but the chief model is clearly the blessing of Joseph's sons by Jacob.

The blessing of Saint Francis

First, we see the version of the blessing as recorded in the *Life of St Francis* by Thomas of Celano:

> When brother Elias sat down on his left side with the other brothers around him, the blessed father crossed his arms and placed his right hand on Elias' head. He had lost the sight and use of his bodily eyes, so he asked: 'Over whom am I holding my right hand?' 'Over brother Elias,' they replied. 'And this is what I wish to do,' he said, 'I bless you, my son, in all and through all, and just as the most High has increased my brothers and sons in your hands, so too, upon you and in you, I bless them all.' (*FA:ED*, vol. 1, p. 276)

Elias was at this time held in good repute by the brothers, as he had been one of the earliest of Francis' companions and was known to be someone Francis trusted. It was Elias who, two years before, had received a vision while sleeping that told of the death of Francis. It was a prediction that Francis took with a remarkably joyful spirit and led to the composing of the 'Canticle of the Creatures'.

Then after this blessing of Elias, Francis turned to all his brothers, and gave them both a warning and a promise. Here he sounded an apocalyptic tone, which became more and more common in the writings of his brothers as the years went by: 'Good-bye, all my sons. Live in the fear of God and remain in him always, for a great test will come upon you and tribulation is drawing near! Happy are those who will persevere in what they have begun' (*FA:ED*, vol. 1, p. 276).

But this wasn't the only story of the passing away of Francis. A later text, known as *The Assisi Compilation*, written between 1244 and 1260, tells it slightly differently. A little earlier, Francis had said to his brothers that he would like to taste one more time the almond cake made by Lady Jacoba dei Settesoli, a holy widow and a great friend of Francis. He asked that they write to her, telling her about his approaching death, but before they could send the letter she appeared at the door. While the friars wondered whether a woman should be allowed into the friars' enclosure, Francis insisted that she be given access to him, calling her 'Brother Jacoba', as if she were an honorary friar. Then Francis remembered that Brother Bernard was also partial to these cakes, so Francis has someone fetch Bernard, who came and sat next to Francis. At first Francis, his eyesight failing, put his right hand on the head of Brother Giles, also sitting next to Francis. But then he realizes that it is not Bernard, and so he places his right hand firmly on Bernard's head. The account concludes:

Blessed Francis, placing his hand on his head, blessed him. 'Write what I tell you,' he then said to one of his companions. 'Brother Bernard was the first brother the Lord gave me. He began first and most perfectly fulfilled the perfection of the holy Gospel, distributing all his goods to the poor. Because of this and his many other prerogatives, I am bound to love him more than any other brother in the whole religion. As much as I am able, it is my will and command that whoever becomes general minister should love and honour him as he would me. Let the other provincial ministers and the brothers of the whole religion hold him in my place.' Because of this, Brother Bernard was greatly consoled as were the other brothers who saw this. (*FA:ED*, vol. 2, pp. 126–7)

In this version of the story two of the earliest companions, Giles and Bernard, take the place of Elias. Bernard in particular was a hero of the friars committed to a literal interpretation of the Franciscan Rule and a strict observance of poverty, a group later known as the 'spirituals'. By the time this account in *The Assisi Compilation* was written, Elias had fallen into disrepute, having been deposed as Minister General in 1239 because of what the brothers saw as his autocratic governance and extravagant lifestyle. Elias was even excommunicated by the pope, though he was ultimately reconciled to the Holy See before his death in 1253.

Around 1245–7, Thomas of Celano wrote a further text on the life of Francis, entitled *The Remembrance of the Desire of a Soul*. In this work, a compilation of stories about Francis gathered from his most faithful companions, Celano adds more details about the death-bed scene. He describes how, covering over with his hand the wound in his side, so as not to arouse the curiosity of those gathered around him, Francis gave his final exhortation: 'I have done what is mine; may Christ teach you what is yours!' (*FA:ED*, vol. 2, p. 386). Although he had had the distraught brothers lay him naked on the naked ground to meet his death, the brother closest to him ensured that he was at least clothed in a poor habit, reassuring him that it was not his possession, and that to wear it was a final act of obedience.

[Francis] then blessed in those who were there, all the other brothers who were living anywhere in the world, and those who were to come after them unto the end of all ages. Let no one claim this blessing as his own for he pronounced it for those absent through those present. As written elsewhere it sounded like something for an individual; instead it should be redirected to the office. (*FA:ED*, vol. 2, p. 387)

This is a slightly awkward recount of the blessing, but it is clearly Thomas of Celano trying to correct the blessing as recorded in his earlier work *The Life of St Francis*. Here in this later text he wants the reader to know that whatever he might have written about Elias earlier was really a blessing for all those in leadership, particularly as Minister General, rather than a personal blessing for the disgraced Brother Elias.

Then Francis blessed his sisters at San Damiano, under the care of Sister Clare, as recorded in *The Assisi Compilation*:

During the week in which blessed Francis died, Lady Clare was seriously ill ... She feared that she would die before blessed Francis. She wept in bitterness of spirit and could not be comforted, because she would not be able before her death to see her only father after God, that is, blessed Francis, her comforter both internally and externally, and her first founder in God's grace ... Blessed Francis considered that what she desired, that is, to see him, could not be done then since they were both seriously ill. To console her, he wrote his blessing in a letter and also absolved her from any failings, if she had any, regarding his commands and wishes, or the commands and wishes of the Son of God. (*FA:ED*, vol. 2, pp. 128–9)

Here we see the tender friendship between Francis and Clare, and how much Francis wanted to lift up Clare's life as an example to his brothers and the whole Church: Clare was to him a model of how to live as a true follower of the calling he himself had been given by God.

Then, after giving his blessings, Francis sang a psalm, and had his 'Canticle of the Creatures' sung by the brothers gathered around him. Finally,

> Even death itself, terrible and hateful to everyone, he exhorted to praise, and going to meet her joyfully, invited her to be his guest, saying: 'Welcome, my Sister Death!' And to the doctor he said: 'Be bold, Brother Doctor, foretell death is near; for to me she will be the gate of Life!' But to the brothers he said: 'When you see I have come to my end put me out naked on the ground as you saw me naked the day before yesterday, and once I am dead, allow me to lie there for as long as it takes to walk a leisurely mile.'
>
> The hour came. All the mysteries of Christ were fulfilled in him, and he happily flew off to God. One of his disciples, a brother of no small fame, saw the soul of the most holy father like a star ascending to heaven, having the immensity of the moon and the brightness of the sun, extending over many waters carried by a little white cloud. (*FA:ED*, vol. 2, p. 388)

Why recount these stories of the passing away of Francis? Partly because they are an intensely moving coda to a symphonic life, a life that breathed fresh air into the Church and society in which Francis lived. He deserved a good ending, an appropriate final scene. But also, the different accounts of his passing raise the questions: Who did Francis bless? What was the vision that he had and which of his followers maintained it most faithfully? Was it Brother Elias, whom he wanted to lead the Order after him and who oversaw the project of building a huge basilica over Francis' tomb? Or were his favourites Bernard and Giles and the other early companions who were daily at his side? Was it Clare and her sisters at San Damiano whom he most wished to bless? Or would he have looked in hope towards any of the other characters we have met in this book: Margaret of Cortona, Bonaventure of Bagnoregio, Angela of Foligno or Jacopone of Todi? Perhaps there is room for them all, each trying to live out with utmost integrity what it meant for them to be Franciscan. It could be said that no one has been able to live up to the pattern of life established by Francis of Assisi, but that doesn't invalidate all those who have done their best to follow in his footsteps. Who could call themselves true followers of Francis? Perhaps the question just remains as an invitation to a renewed commitment to Jesus and the gospel: '... the kingdom of God has come near. Repent and believe in the good news' (Mark 1.15). Francis asks of us nothing more, and nothing less, and offers us all his blessing by which he ends his 'Letter to the Entire Order' (*FA:ED*, vol. 1, pp. 120–1):

Almighty, eternal, just and merciful God,
give us miserable ones
the grace to do for you alone
what we know you want us to do
and always to desire what pleases you.
Inwardly cleansed,
interiorly enlightened
and inflamed by the fire of the Holy Spirit,
may we be able to follow
in the footprints of your beloved Son,
our Lord Jesus Christ,
and, by Your grace alone,
may we make our way to you,
Most High,
who live and rule
in perfect Trinity and simple Unity,
and are glorified
God almighty,
forever and ever.
Amen.

Bibliography

All quotations from the works of Francis and the early documents are taken from *Francis of Assisi: Early Documents* (abbreviated here as *FA:ED*), edited by Regis J. Armstrong, J. A. Wayne Hellmann and William J. Short (Hyde Park, NY: New City Press, 1999–2001): Volume 1 *The Saint*; Volume 2 *The Founder*; Volume 3 *The Prophet*. Quotations from these volumes are given as volume number and page number in the text.

Angela of Foligno, 1993, *The Book of Blessed Angela of Foligno* in *Angela of Foligno: Complete Works*, Classics of Western Spirituality, translated, with an introduction, by Paul Lachance OFM, Mahwah, NJ: Paulist Press.

Armstrong, Edward A., 1973, *Saint Francis: Nature Mystic – The Derivation and Significance of the Nature Stories in the Franciscan Legend*, Berkeley: University of California Press.

Armstrong, Regis J., 2006, *Clare of Assisi: Early Documents (CA:ED)*, *The Lady*, Hyde Park, NY: New City Press.

Bartoli, Marco, 2010, *Saint Clare: Beyond the Legend*, translated by Sister Frances Teresa Downing OSC, Cincinnati: St. Anthony Messenger Press.

Bell, Rudolph, 1985, *Holy Anorexia*, Chicago: University of Chicago Press.

Bernard of Clairvaux, 1987, *Selected Works*, translation by G. R. Evans, Classics of Western Spirituality, Mahwah, NJ: Paulist Press.

Bevegnati, Fra Giunta, 2012, *The Life and Miracles of Saint Margaret of Cortona*, translation and introduction by Thomas Renna, edited by Shannon Larson, St. Bonaventure University, NY: Franciscan Institute Publications.

Bonaventure, 1960, 'The Triple Way or Love Enkindled', 'The Tree of Life', 'The Mystical Vine', 'On the Perfection of Life Addressed to Sisters', from *The Works of Bonaventure: Vol.1, Mystical Opuscula*, translated by José de Vinck, Quincy, IL: Franciscan Press.

——— 1963, *The Breviloquium, The Works of Bonaventure*, Vol. 2, translated by José de Vinck, Paterson, NJ: St. Anthony Guild Press.

——— 1970, *Collations on the Six Days, The Works of Bonaventure*, Vol. 5, translated by José de Vinck, Paterson, NJ: St. Anthony Guild Press.

——— 1978, *Bonaventure: The Soul's Journey into God; The Tree of Life; The Life of St. Francis*, translation and introduction by Ewert Cousins, Classics of Western Spirituality, London: SPCK.

——— 1994, *Writings Concerning the Franciscan Order*, Works of Saint Bonaventure, vol. 5, translation with introduction and commentary by Dominic Monti OFM, St. Bonaventure University, NY: Franciscan Institute Publications.

——— 1996, *St. Bonaventure's On the Reduction of the Arts to Theology*, Works of Saint Bonaventure, vol. 1, translation with introduction and commentary by Zachary Hayes OFM, St. Bonaventure University, NY: Franciscan Institute Publications.

——— 2002, *Itinerarium Mentis in Deum, The Soul's Journey into God*, Works of St. Bonaventure, Vol. 2, revised and expanded, edited by Philotheus Boehner OFM and Zachary Hayes OFM, St. Bonaventure University, NY: Franciscan Institute Publications.

——— 2013, *Commentary on the Sentences: Philosophy of God*, Works of St. Bonaventure, vol. 16, translation, introduction and notes by R. E. Houser and Timothy B. Noone, St. Bonaventure University, NY: Franciscan Institute Publications.

——— 2018, *Hexaemeron, Conferences on the Six Days of Creation: The Illuminations of the Church*, Works of St. Bonaventure, vol. 18, translation, introduction and notes by Jay M. Hammond, St. Bonaventure University, NY: Franciscan Institute Publications.

Brooke, Rosalind B., 1959, *Early Franciscan Government*, Cambridge: Cambridge University Press.

——— (ed. and trans.), 1970, *Scripta Leonis, Rufini et Angeli Sociorum S. Francisci: The Writings of Leo, Rufino and Angelo, Companions of St. Francis*, Oxford: Clarendon Press.

Bornstein, Daniel, 'The Uses of the Body: The Church and the Cult of Santa Margherita da Cortona', *Church History*, vol. 62, no. 2 (June 1993), pp. 163–77.

Burr, David, 2001, *The Spiritual Franciscans: From Protest to Persecution in the Century After Saint Francis*, University Park, PA: The Pennsylvania State University Press.

Bynum, Caroline Walker, 1982, *Jesus as Mother: Studies in the spirituality of the High Middle Ages*, Berkeley, CA: University of California Press.

——— 1987, *Holy Feast and Holy Fast: The Religious Significance of*

Food to Medieval Women, Berkeley, CA: University of California Press.

Carney, Margaret, OSF, 2021, *Light of Assisi: The Story of Saint Clare*, Cincinnati, OH: Franciscan Media.

Carpenter, Charles, 1999, *Theology as the Road to Holiness in St. Bonaventure*, Mahwah, NJ: Paulist Press.

The Cloud of Unknowing, 1961, anonymous, translated by Clifton Wolters, London: Penguin.

Coakley, John W., 2006, *Women, Men, & Spiritual Power: Female Saints & Their Male Collaborators*, New York: Columbia University Press.

——, 'Gender and the Authority of Friars: The Significance of Holy Women for Thirteenth-century Franciscans and Dominicans', *Church History*, vol. 60, no. 4 (December 1991), pp. 445–60.

Cocksedge, Simon, Samuel Double and Nicholas Alan Worssam, 2021, *Seeing Differently: Franciscans and Creation*, Norwich: Canterbury Press.

Consiglio, Cyprian, 2010, *Prayer in the Cave of the Heart: The Universal Call to Contemplation*, Collegeville, MN: Liturgical Press.

Cuthbert, Father, OFM Cap, 1900, *A Tuscan Penitent: The Life and Legend of St. Margaret of Cortona*, London: Burns, Oates & Washbourne (translation altered slightly).

Dalarun, Jacques, 2016, *The Canticle of Brother Sun: Francis of Assisi Reconciled*, translated by Philippe Yates, St. Bonaventure University, NY: Franciscan Institute Publications.

Delio, Ilia, OSF, 2001, *Simply Bonaventure: An Introduction to His Life, Thought, and Writings*, Hyde Park, NY: New City Press.

Dickens, Andrea Janelle, 2009, *The Female Mystic: Great Women Thinkers of the Middle Ages*, London: I.B. Tauris.

Doyno, Mary Harvey, 'The Creation of a Franciscan Lay Saint: Margaret of Cortona and her *Legenda*', *Past & Present*, no. 228 (August 2015), pp. 57–91.

Dreyer, Elizabeth A., 2005, *Passionate Spirituality: Hildegard of Bingen and Hadewijch of Brabant*, Hyde Park, NY: Paulist Press.

Eckhart, Meister, 1994, *Selected Writings*, translated by Oliver Davies, London: Penguin.

Fonck, Benet A., OFM, 1996, *To Cling With All Her Heart to Him: The Spirituality of St. Clare of Assisi*, Quincy: Franciscan Press.

Frances Teresa, OSC, 1995, *This Living Mirror: Reflections on Clare of Assisi*, London: Darton, Longman & Todd.

Gallyon, Margaret, 2000, *The Visions, Revelations and Teachings of Angela of Foligno: A Member of the Third Order of St Francis*, Brighton: The Alpha Press.

Giles of Assisi, 1990, *Golden Words: The Sayings of Brother Giles*, with a biography by Nello Vian, translated by Ivo O'Sullivan, Chicago, IL: Franciscan Herald Press.

Gooder, Paula R., 2006, *Only the Third Heaven? 2 Corinthians 12.1–10 and Heavenly Ascent*, Library of New Testament Studies, London: Bloomsbury / T&T Clark.

Goorbergh, Edith A. Van OSC and Theodore H. Zweerman OFM, 2000, *Light Shining Through a Veil: On Saint Clare's Letters to Saint Agnes of Prague*, translated by Aline Looman-Graaskamp and Frances Teresa OSC, Leuven: Peeters.

Gregory of Nyssa, 1978, *The Life of Moses*, translation by Abraham J. Malherbe and Everett Ferguson, Classics of Western Spirituality, Ramsey, NJ: Paulist Press.

Habig, Marion A. (ed.), 1972, *St. Francis of Assisi: Writings and Early Biographies, English Omnibus of the Sources for the Life of St. Francis*, London: SPCK.

Hadewijch: The Complete Works, 1980, translated by Mother Columba Hart OSB, Classics of Western Spirituality, Mahwah, NJ: Paulist Press.

Hammond, Jay M. (ed.), 2004, *Francis of Assisi – History, Hagiography and Hermeneutics in the Early Documents*, Hyde Park, NY: New City Press.

Hammond, Jay M., J. A. Wayne Hellman and Jared Goff (eds), 2014, *A Companion to Bonaventure*, Leiden: Brill.

Hayes, Zachary, OFM, 1992, *The Hidden Centre: Spirituality and Speculative Christology in St. Bonaventure*, St. Bonaventure University, NY: Franciscan Institute Publications.

——, 1999, *Bonaventure: Mystical Writings*, New York: Crossroad.

Helen Julian, CSF, 2020, *Franciscan Footprints: Following Christ in the ways of Francis and Clare*, Abingdon: Bible Reading Fellowship.

Hollywood, Amy and Patricia Z. Beckman (eds), 2012, *The Cambridge Companion to Christian Mysticism*, Cambridge: Cambridge University Press.

Horan, Daniel, P., 2021, *The Way of the Franciscans: A Prayer Journey Through Lent*, London: SPCK.

House, Adrian, 2000, *Francis of Assisi*, London: Pimlico.

Hugo, William R., 2011, *Studying the life of Saint Francis of Assisi – a beginner's workbook*, second edition, Hyde Park, NY: New City Press.

Isaac the Syrian, 2011, *Ascetical Homilies of Saint Isaac the Syrian*, translated from the Greek and Syriac by the Holy Transfiguration Monastery, revised second edition, Boston, MA; Homily 77.

Jacopone da Todi, 1982, *Jacopone da Todi: The Lauds*, translated by Serge and Elizabeth Hughes, Classics of Western Spirituality, Ramsey, NJ: Paulist Press.

Jansen, Katherine L., 'The Meaning of the Magdalen for Female Penitents of Later Medieval Italy', *Memoirs of the American Academy in Rome*, Vol. 45 (2000), pp. 131–52.

Johnson, Timothy J., 2000, *The Soul in Ascent: Bonaventure on Poverty, Prayer, and Union with God*, Quincy, IL: Franciscan Press.

Julian of Norwich, 1998, *Revelations of Divine Love*, translated by Elizabeth Spearing, London: Penguin.

Knox, Lezlie S., 2008, *Creating Clare of Assisi: Female Franciscan Identities in Later Medieval Italy*, Leiden: Brill.

Lachance, Paul and Pierre Brunette, 2015, *The Earliest Franciscans: The Legacy of Giles of Assisi, Roger of Provence, and James of Milan*, compiled by Paul Lachance and Pierre Brunette, translated by Kathryn Krug, Classics of Western Spirituality, Mahwah, NY: Paulist Press.

Lamm, Julia A., 2013, *The Wiley Blackwell Companion to Christian Mysticism*, Oxford: Wiley Blackwell.

Lao Tsu, 1973, *Tao Te Ching*, translated by Gia-Fu Feng and Jane English, London: Wildwood House Ltd.

Leclerc, Eloi, OFM, 1977, *The Canticle of Creatures: Symbols of Union*, translated by Matthew J. O'Connell, Chicago, IL: Franciscan Herald Press.

Mazzoni, Cristina, 1999, *Angela of Foligno: Memorial*, translation by John Cirignano, The Library of Medieval Women, Cambridge: D.S. Brewer.

McGinn, Bernard, 1998, *The Flowering of Mysticism: Men and Women in the New Mysticism – 1200–1350*, The Presence of God: A History of Western Christian Mysticism Volume 3, New York: Crossroad.

Moloney, Brian, 2013, *Francis of Assisi and His Canticle of Brother Sun Reassessed*, New York: Palgrave Macmillan.

Mooney, Catherine M., 1994, 'The Authorial Role of Brother A. in the Composition of Angela of Foligno's Revelations' in E. Ann Matter and John Coakley (eds), *Creative Women in Medieval and Early Modern Italy: A Religious and Artistic Renaissance*, Philadelphia: University of Pennsylvania Press, pp. 34–63.

——, 1999, '*Imitatio Christi* or *Imitatio Mariae*? Clare of Assisi and Her Interpreters' in Catherine M. Mooney (ed.), *Gendered Voices: Medieval Saints and their Interpreters*, Philadelphia, PA: University of Pennsylvania Press, pp. 52–77.

——, 2016, *Clare of Assisi and the Thirteenth-century Church: Religious Women, Rules, and Resistance*, Philadelphia, PA: University of Pennsylvania Press.

Moorman, John, 1968, *A History of the Franciscan Order: From Its Origins to the Year 1517*, Oxford: Clarendon Press.

Mueller, Joan, 2010, *A Companion to Clare of Assisi: Life, Writings, and Spirituality*, Leiden: Brill.

Murray, Wendy, 2020, *Clare of Assisi: Gentle Warrior*, Brewster, MA: Paraclete Press.

Newman, Barbara, 'Annihilation and Authorship: Three Women Mystics of the 1290s', *Speculum*, vol. 91, no. 3 (July 2016), pp. 591–630.

Osborne, Kenan B., OFM (ed.), 1994, *The History of Franciscan Theology*, St. Bonaventure University, NY: Franciscan Institute Publications.

Pazzelli, Raffaele, 1989, *St. Francis and the Third Order*, Chicago, IL: Franciscan Herald Press.

Peck, George T., 1980, *The Fool of God: Jacopone da Todi*, Tuscaloosa, AL: The University of Alabama Press.

Pitchford, Susan, 2006, *Following Francis: The Franciscan Way for Everyone*, Harrisburg, PA: Morehouse.

Porete, Marguerite, 1993, *The Mirror of Simple Souls*, translated and introduced by Ellen L. Babinsky, Classics of Western Spirituality, Mahwah, NJ: Paulist Press.

Ramon, Brother, SSF, 1994, *Franciscan Spirituality: Following Saint Francis Today*, London: SPCK.

Robson, Michael J. P. (ed.), 2012, *The Cambridge Companion to Francis of Assisi*, Cambridge: Cambridge University Press.

Rohr, Richard, OFM, 2014, *Eager to Love: The Alternative Way of Francis of Assisi*, London: Hodder & Stoughton.

Rolle, Richard, 1972, *The Fire of Love*, translated by Clifton Wolters, London: Penguin.

Rout, Paul, 1996, *Francis and Bonaventure*, London: Fount.

Scholl, Edith, OCSO, 2009, *Words for the Journey: A Monastic Vocabulary*, Collegeville, MN: Cistercian Publications / Liturgical Press.

Şenocak, Neslihan, 2012, *The Poor and the Perfect: The Rise of Learning in the Franciscan Order, 1209–1310*, Ithaca, NY: Cornell University Press.

Sheldrake, Philip, 2005, *The New SCM Dictionary of Christian Spirituality*, London: SCM Press.

Short, William J., OFM, 1999, *Poverty and Joy: The Franciscan Tradition*, London: Darton, Longman & Todd.

Sorrell, Roger D., 1988, *St. Francis of Assisi and Nature: Tradition and Innovation in Western Christian Attitudes toward the Environment*, Oxford: Oxford University Press.

Thompson, Augustine, 2012, *Francis of Assisi – a New Biography*, Ithaca, NY: Cornell University Press.

Underhill, Evelyn, 1911, *Mysticism*, London: Methuen & Co. Ltd.

———, 1919, *Jacopone da Todi, Poet and Mystic 1228–1306: A Spiritual Biography*, London: J.M. Dent & Sons (translation altered slightly).

———, 1925, *The Mystics of the Church*, London: James Clarke.

Vauchez, Andre, 2012, *Francis of Assisi: The Life and Afterlife of a Medieval Saint*, London: Yale University Press.

Venuti, Lawrence, 'Translating Jacopone da Todi: Archaic Poetries and Modern Audiences' in *Translation and Literature*, vol. 12, no. 2 (2003), pp. 231–51.

Vettori, Alessandro, 2004, *Poets of Divine Love: Franciscan Mystical Poetry of the Thirteenth Century*, New York: Fordham University Press.

Williams, J. P., 2018, *Seeking the God Beyond: A Beginner's Guide to Christian Apophatic Spirituality*, London: SCM Press.

Williams, Rowan Clare, 2003, *A Condition of Complete Simplicity: Franciscan Wisdom for Today's World*, Norwich: Canterbury Press.

Wroe, Anne, 2018, *Francis: A Life in Songs*, London: Jonathan Cape.

Appendix

Questions for reflection and discussion

1 How would you summarize the message of St Francis in a single sentence?
What was distinctive about his teaching?
Which aspect of his teaching is most relevant to the world today?

2 In what way was Clare true to the inspiration of Francis?
Was being enclosed in a monastery a hindrance to being a Franciscan? Why?
What did Francis and Clare value in each other?

3 Which aspect of the teaching of Francis did Giles communicate best?
Are 'ecstasy' or 'rapture' valid or even important aspects of prayer?
How do you find it easiest to pray?

4 To what extent is liturgy a form of drama? Was Margaret overly dramatic?
What place should fasting have in the Christian life?
Is it helpful to have a spiritual director or someone to hear confessions?

5 What was the core of Bonaventure's teaching?
How important is study in the spiritual life?
Which Christian authors have you found most helpful?

6 If someone like Angela came to your church next Sunday, what reception would she get?
Does the 'negative way' resonate with your own experience?
Do you have a sense of God talking to you?

7 Is it important to consider our mortality? Why?
Who in today's world could be compared with Jacopone?
Would you call yourself a Franciscan? Why?